THE PRESIDENT WORE SPATS

The President Wore Spats

A BIOGRAPHY OF GLENN FRANK

———◆———

LAWRENCE H. LARSEN

MADISON
THE STATE HISTORICAL SOCIETY OF WISCONSIN
MCMLXV

Copyright © 1965 by

THE STATE HISTORICAL SOCIETY OF WISCONSIN

LIBRARY OF CONGRESS CATALOG CARD NUMBER: LC 65-63009

Europe: W. S. Hall & Co., Inc., Amsterdam, London, New York
Canada: Harvest House, Ltd., Montreal
India: Thacker & Co., Ltd., Bombay

Printed in the United States of America by
WORZALLA PUBLISHING COMPANY
STEVENS POINT ● WISCONSIN

To Barbara

PREFACE

GLENN FRANK was a colorful and multi-faceted man, and few who met him came away with a neutral impression. His admirers thought him a dedicated economic thinker who devoted much of his life to explaining how the United States could best adjust to the problems of urban industrialism. His critics considered him a crass and shallow opportunist who was interested solely in his own aggrandizement. As is usually the case, the truth lay somewhere in between.

He was affable and intelligent, and despite the rather pompous facade which he presented in public, even his detractors admitted that he was a fluent speaker and a congenial companion. He proved himself to be a capable and energetic administrator in a wide variety of positions, and he seemed to thrive on hard work and a tight, overcrowded schedule. He was certainly not a thinker—his hectic pace allowed little time for relaxation, much less for introspection—yet in his own way he was a serious student of public affairs. Above all he was a promoter, a suave and articulate salesman who was at his best when he had an audience before him. Had he chosen to do so, he could probably have parlayed a vacant lot into a metropolis or a pushcart into a vast corporation. He chose instead to promote an even less promising commodity: a poor boy from a tiny hamlet in northeastern Missouri—himself. That he succeeded as well as he did was both a tribute to his promotional ability and a commentary on the era in which he lived.

Glenn Frank was an apt spokesman for the America of the 1920's. Like thousands of other self-made men, he was glib and acquisitive, and he made a substantial fortune from his multifarious activities as editor, author, and lecturer.

But at the same time he deplored the naked materialism of the postwar world and espoused a program of enlightened capitalism which quickly captured the ear of the American business community. The resolution of labor-management strife, the modernization of religion, the abolition of war, the reform of higher education—all, Frank said, could be achieved under the leadership of "business statesmen," rather than that of self-seeking politicians or vicious demagogues. There was nothing particularly daring or even original in his philosophy, but he set it forth so clearly and forcefully that he became one of the nation's best-known prophets of benevolent capitalism. His message was perfectly suited to soothing the fears and salving the conscience of a business community long beset by grumbling workers and carping critics.

In the end, of course, Frank's very success betrayed him. In 1925 he attained the presidency of the University of Wisconsin—not because of any demonstrated capacity for educational administration, but because his rhetoric had dazzled the University's regents. For several years he succeeded in a very difficult role, healing old political wounds, dealing effectively with the state legislature, courting the alumni, promoting the University throughout the nation, and carrying out bold experimental programs in higher education. But when the giddiness of the 1920's gave way to the bleak Depression years, Frank's bland optimism began to wear thin, and his weaknesses—personal as well as intellectual—stood out in bold relief. Finally he was cast aside, and rather brutally, as if the University were now embarrassed with having chosen him in the first place. He spent the last years of his life in trying to reattain the early promise of his career. But in this, too, Frank failed, his life cut short by a tragic accident.

I hope that this biography will shed new light on Glenn Frank's checkered career. I first became interested in him while working as a graduate assistant in the University of Wisconsin Archives during 1955 and 1956, and ultimately my interest led me to write a doctoral dissertation on Frank which serves as the basis for this book. Many people gave me encouragement and assistance along the way, but my greatest debts are to David Shannon, who directed the dissertation, and to the late Howard K. Beale, under whom it was originally begun. Jesse Boell provided valuable leads about the operation of the University of Wisconsin during Frank's tenure as president, as did Vernon Carstensen, Mark Ingraham, and others. Charles N. Glaab, James Remley, Wayne Larsen, and Dennis Bodem read portions of the manuscript; Jonathan Spurgeon, William Petrowski, and David Healy all offered succinct criticism. The staffs of the various libraries and archives which I visited were invariably courteous and efficient, and my wife Barbara typed the manuscript and patiently bore my fits of temper when things were not going well during the process of writing it.

LAWRENCE H. LARSEN

University of Missouri at Kansas City
Autumn, 1964

CONTENTS

ILLUSTRATIONS

A selection of pictures illustrating
various phases of Glenn Frank's career
follows pages 54 and 126.

I

The Road to Green Bay

THE LATE MODEL FORD SEDAN roared swiftly down Wisconsin Highway 57 towards Green Bay. Its headlights cut a yellowish swath through the gathering darkness of a cool, late summer evening. There were three people in the automobile. The driver—a dark, handsome youth only a year out of Harvard University—kept the accelerator near the floorboards. As the speed of the car increased he peered ahead, trying to see beyond the range of the lights. Beside him sat his fifty-two-year-old father, dapper and immaculately dressed, lost in thought as he penciled notes on the back of a used envelope. In the rear seat a sound technician slept fitfully amid a clutter of loud-speaker equipment. Thousands of people throughout Wisconsin would have recognized the older man in the front seat. The large red and white posters on the sides of the vehicle proclaimed him "GLENN FRANK, REPUBLICAN FOR U. S. SENATOR." The date, Sunday, September 15, 1940, was only two days before the primary election.

Glenn Frank was already an hour late for his speaking engagement, and he was in a hurry. Some of the distinguished politicians and businessmen gathered in the ballroom of Green Bay's Belmont Hotel would contribute money to his campaign, and he did not wish to keep them waiting longer

3

than necessary. He had telephoned from a gas station in Chilton, thirty-eight miles from Green Bay, to explain that the automobile's lights had started blinking. Following repairs, he said, "We'll be there in as long a time as sixty miles an hour will take. You fellows go ahead and eat without us . . . ."

During the weeks of electioneering that lay behind, Glenn Frank had learned to take in stride the unavoidable disruptions of schedule, the apologetic telephone calls, and the inevitable trips over the speed limit. He was not a professional politician, and in the beginning he had been unaccustomed to the rigors of running for office. But by now he was a seasoned veteran of the political battlefield, used to shaking hands, eating drab banquet fare, attending countless party functions, and delivering partisan speeches.

He faced long odds in the race for the Senate seat. Six other candidates sought the Republican nomination, but for strategic reasons Frank treated them with indifference.[1] Exhibiting confidence, he campaigned against the man whom he considered would be his opponent in November: Robert M. La Follette, Jr., the Progressive incumbent, son of the most famous political leader in the state's history and brother of Philip Fox La Follette, a former governor and a power to be reckoned with in Wisconsin. Time and again Frank claimed that the La Follettes were "at heart fascist" and that their National Progressive party represented "nothing more than small scale totalitarianism." "I have myself felt the heavy fist of the La Follette dictatorship," he asserted. "If you make me your nominee . . . , I promise you to leave no stone unturned to rid Wisconsin forever of the latter-day La Follettism and to stand four-square in the United States Senate against the Hitlerization of America."

He had carried this message across the length and breadth of the state. He had stressed it in the shadow of grain elevators on the Superior waterfront and in the main streets of Mosinee, Park Falls, and Lancaster. He had expounded it to workers before grimy factory gates in Racine, West Allis, and Kenosha, and to industrialists and financiers in paneled Milwaukee board rooms. He had recorded it for the radio in hot, stuffy studios in Eau Claire and Sheboygan. And apparently his remorseless attacks had succeeded. The public opinion polls indicated that he would win the nomination and perhaps go on to unseat La Follette in the November election.

Yet even though all signs pointed to a primary victory, Frank pressed his campaign right up until election eve. As his son commented wearily, "With eight to twelve speeches every day, you have to keep it down to the floorboards all the time." So, as the car sped along the highway from Stoughton, southeast of Madison, where Frank had addressed an enthusiastic crowd at a farm festival, the candidate mulled over yet another speech. In keeping with long-established habit, Frank waited until the last possible moment to put something down on paper. In addition to denouncing the La Follettes, he decided to depict Franklin D. Roosevelt as an anti-business President. He would claim that the New Deal had not invented intelligence, conscience, and humanitarianism, nor had it invented a sense of social responsibility. Hungry men could not eat political promises, and the world had neither ended in 1929 nor begun in 1933. Glenn Frank never finished composing his speech.

Fifteen miles from Green Bay a rise loomed up in the highway. Over the crest the road turned sharply to the right, where it formed a Y-shaped junction with a secondary road. Between the diverging roadways, maintenance men had stored a large pile of sand. Young Glenn took the rise at high speed. He saw the curve, slammed on the brakes, and wrestled desperately with the steering wheel. But it was too late. The Ford skidded, careened onto its left side, and glanced off the sand pile. It rolled over and over, landing on its top in a broken heap sixty feet beyond. The force of the crash hurled the boy through the windshield, and he died shortly afterwards. The sound technician, thrown clear of the wreck, received serious injuries. The elder Frank remained in the front seat, trapped under the smashed top. He died instantly of a broken neck.[2]

The report of the accident soon reached Green Bay. The reception at the Belmont Hotel, gay in anticipation of meeting the candidate, quickly dissolved in silent horror. Teletype messages and radio bulletins flashed the news. Frank's wife, Mary, learned of the tragedy at the family home in Maple Bluff, a suburb of Madison. Young Glenn's fiancee heard of it in a dormitory at Milwaukee's Downer College. The next day Wisconsin newspapers headlined Glenn Frank's death. Long obituaries traced his meteoric career: his humble Midwestern birth, his evangelistic work, his days as Northwestern University's first alumni secretary, his position as adviser to a wealthy Eastern philanthropist, his editorship of the *Century Magazine* and of *Rural Progress,* his activities as a public lecturer and a nationally syndicated columnist, his presidency of the University of Wisconsin, and his rising prominence in the Republican party. Other aspects of Frank's multi-faceted career were also noticed in the press. The public debates which had characterized his twelve-year tenure as president of the University of Wisconsin—ranging from disputes over free love and drugged football players to his last, bitter struggle with the University Regents—received full coverage. In death as in life Glenn Frank provoked discussion and controversy.[3]

Associates, political opponents, educators, newspaper columnists, and people who had never met him lamented his tragic death. Organizations eulogized him at elaborate banquets. Countless editorials praised his contributions, and legislators, many of whom had criticized his actions, now lauded him unstintingly in a memorial resolution. The faculty of the University of Wisconsin honored his memory. Throughout the state, people attested to his intelligence, devotion to principle, sportsmanship, honest political ambitions, and unfailing concern for the welfare of his family.[4]

The tragedy cast a pall over the primary election. Wisconsin voters went to the polls while the "two Glenns" lay in state in the flower-bedecked rotunda of the State Capitol. In death Frank ran third in the election, and more than forty thousand voters, in curious tribute, marked his name on the ballot. Then, almost as quickly as he had achieved his measure of fame, people forgot him. His often perceptive comments on national and world events no longer appeared in the newspapers; his grandiloquent speeches no longer captivated radio and banquet audiences. And so a man who had thrilled tens of thousands with his speeches, who had counted among his friends many national literary, business, and political personalities, and who had become one of the most controversial figures ever associated with the University of Wisconsin, disappeared from the scene. No plaques were erected in his memory; no buildings were to bear his name. Within twenty years of his passing only a few people—old friends and bitter enemies—remembered him well. But once the old had been young, once Frank had administered the University of Wisconsin, and once he had seemed to stand on the threshold of fame.

Glenn Frank had gone far. He had escaped from the confining atmosphere of northeastern Missouri, a rural region wholly lacking the cultural advantages and economic opportunities of large cities. Except for Kirksville, a marketing center with a population of some five thousand, the few towns in the area—Glenwood, Queen City, Kahoka, Bethel, Chapel, Possum, and Green Top—were little more than names on a map. Frank had grown up in a stable agricultural community where the vast majority of the inhabitants lived on farms which had been in their families since the 1840's and 1850's. Almost everyone was white, Anglo-Saxon, and Protestant. They owned their land, toiled long hours, and believed that God rewarded those who worked with their hands. The rolling prairie, rich in alluvial soil and well watered, provided a fair return, and few farmers were poor, though most had little spare cash to spend on luxuries. They took for granted kerosene lighting, wood-burning stoves, linoleum carpeting, worn furniture, well water, and clapboard privies.

Until he was almost twenty-three years of age, Glenn Frank had few direct contacts with the outside world. Born in Queen City on October 1, 1887, he grew up in nearby Green Top, a town promoter's dusty failure. Green Top's reason for continuing existence was a gloomy railroad station which served as a local shipping point for farm produce. Except on paper, the town had never fulfilled its promoter's hopes, and in this as in most other respects it differed but little from the other towns in the area. The hundred residents lived in a cluster of white frame houses, shaded by uneven rows of elms and oaks. Most of them belonged to one or the other of the town's two churches, and they practiced their religion with evangelical fervor. The village schoolhouse functioned also as a community center, and what passed for a business district consisted of a gravel street lined with two drug stores, a grocery that included a post office, another grocery that sold hardware, a couple of general mercantile firms, and the inevitable furniture and undertaking establishment. On Friday and Saturday nights Green Top came to life for a few hours, as farm families came to shop and to idle on the street corners exchanging news. During the rest of the week only the sound of an occasional carriage or the clangor of a steam locomotive broke the stillness.[5]

Some Americans who emerged from similar localities felt cheated by the confining atmosphere and limited challenges of small-town life. They recalled only stifling prejudice, narrow thinking, and rigid conformity. Hamlin Garland wrote bitterly of wasted years in a village in southeastern Wisconsin; Sinclair Lewis found little to commend of life in a small Minnesota community. But Glenn Frank, with nostalgic enthusiasm, consistently extolled life in rural Missouri. According to him, the Green Tops of America were the best places to experience the dynamics of the American political experiment and to see people demonstrating their capacity for self-government. "My memory," Frank said, "conjures up the picture of a midwestern village post office, in which, as a boy, I spent many fascinating hours," observing the democratic give and take at what was essentially the "meeting place of the village mind." The post office was the forum where men wearing "hand-me-down clothes" exhibited original and independent thinking in the vigorous debates which fashioned "neighborhood opinion."[6]

Whether or not Frank truly believed this pastoral idyl, he did know how to capitalize upon the mythology of his background. It was helpful for a man of ambition to emphasize a rural past. In an age in which urban politics was virtually synonymous with corruption, this legacy of cracker-barrel democracy, with its underlying assumption of rural virtue, impressed many Americans who had not themselves grown up in a rural environment. Despite Frank's avowed enthusiasm, however, he apparently never regretted having left Green Top. Like so many self-made men who escaped the prairie environment, Glenn Frank romanticized his homely background. Yet throughout his career he steadfastly ignored correspondence from people whom he had known in his youth, and he returned to Green Top only rarely and then only for the shortest of visits.

He was by fifteen years the youngest of four sons of Gordon and Nancy Hombs Frank, who were forty-three and thirty-four years of age respectively at the time of his birth. Gordon Frank, a country schoolteacher, never earned a large salary. To his son Glenn he represented "a good name, a clean life, a record of honor unsullied, an eager interest in books and ideas, and a sense of social responsibility" rather than love and affection. Frank remembered his mother quite differently. He said that she was a person of rare devoutness who "discharged her priestly ministry to us with an art that wholly concealed its art, although I am sure she was quite unaware of her artistry in motherhood."[7]

Nancy Frank, a Methodist who bordered on religious fanaticism, liked to describe, with a relish that few people ever forgot, her fifteen hours of suffering prior to Glenn's birth. She instilled in her son a strong belief in God and a love of books, but she pampered him badly, protecting him from his older brothers and encouraging him to draw attention to himself. "When he was only six or seven he used to get on a chair and make us all listen," one of his brothers said. "And when he got through he'd get down and pass the hat. We had to put something in, too, you bet. And we didn't dare laugh, no sir. Glenn was always mighty touchy that way."[8] For his discourses he drew upon the Bible and on what he learned in school. Completely uninhibited, he once interrupted a church supper to deliver a "sermonette." He burst forth anywhere and at any time. "When Glenn was just a squirt," said one who knew him well, "he never did anything when he was a boy but keep a-reading and a-talking. At least, I never heard tell of him doing a day's work."[9]

When Frank was twelve years old he became a boy evangelist, largely through the influence of a Methodist minister, Frederick Smith, one of many revivalists engaged in saving souls in Green Top and other Missouri towns. Smith, a former Northwestern University football player, appealed directly to youth with sermons that emphasized the connection between religion and modern times. Frank imitated his manner and quoted his sermons. Upon discovering that the youth expressed himself fluently and showed an interest in religion, Smith cultivated the Frank family and persuaded them to allow their son to accompany him on a summer tour. On the circuit, Smith exploited his protégé to the fullest. Frank delivered as many as six sermons a day, sometimes riding over thirty miles at a stretch on horseback through the oppressive summer heat. Still, he enjoyed every minute of it. He had never traveled before—not even to surrounding counties—and like most boys his age, he liked the excitement and satisfaction of speaking before attentive listeners. Although he saw few of the dimes and quarters dropped in Reverend Smith's collection plates, he returned home imbued with a missionary spirit.[10]

The summer's experiences and his mother's urging convinced young Glenn to pursue a career as a Methodist minister. He proposed to follow in Smith's footsteps: a Methodist institution such as Northwestern University, then divinity school. All this would take time and money. Meanwhile, he was determined not to abandon religion. During the next few years he spent his days in school studying English grammar, American literature, composition, rhetoric, plane and solid geometry, and algebra, and his nights at home learning the rudiments of Methodism. Finally, in December, 1903, shortly after his sixteenth birthday, he appeared before the Conference of the Kirksville District of the Annual Conference of the Methodist Northern Missouri Conference. After answering a series of questions about the Scriptures and theological dogma, he received a license as a Local Preacher, an authority which gave him wide freedom of action. The Conference renewed his license each year until 1912, and under it Frank performed most of the functions and obligations usually associated only with an ordained Methodist minister.[11]

He soon put his license to use. After graduating from high school in the spring of 1904 he became a circuit rider, although he was then only seventeen. His calling consisted of six small congregations in the crossroads communities of Bethel, Millard, Wesley, Chapel, Possum, and Hollow. For three years he delivered sermons in three of those places every Sunday, covering the distance between on horseback. In 1907 he was promoted to a church in Kahoka and a year later he moved on to an even better position in Glenwood. Tending to the needs of those whom he called "spiritual invalids" kept him busy.[12] There were picnics and dinners to attend, funeral sermons to preach, sick calls to make, sinners to save, marriages to perform, and broken homes to patch. His parishioners felt that despite his youth he demonstrated conspicuous ability. They considered him an exceptional young man, gifted with a good command of the language and a forceful delivery, who would one day occupy an eminent position in the clergy. Yet in spite of the praise which Frank's audiences lavished on him, his income was meager. To make ends meet he held a variety of part-time jobs, ranging from pitching hay to painting signs. And, under

these circumstances, preaching gradually lost its glamour.[13]
In the course of his preaching duties Frank learned to prepare sermons and perfected his speaking delivery. To compensate for his lack of formal training he listened to speeches or sermons at every opportunity, read books on rhetoric and elocution, and even practiced voice control on barnyard animals. Through trial and error he developed an effective but unpretentious method. He relied on tone and diction rather than on the arm-waving widely used at the time. Preparing his homilies proved far easier. He culled material from various religious books, including *The World's Great Sermons* by Glenville Kleiser, *Revival Addresses* by R. A. Torrey, *Selected Sermons* by T. DeWitt Talmadge, and the *Expositions of Holy Scripture,* a twelve-volume work printed by a Methodist publishing house in New York. He compiled his sermons by relying heavily on his intuitive capacity for selecting catchy, vivid, and graphic sentences well suited to his style of delivery. As he became more accomplished, both in selection and delivery, he found that he could enthrall a congregation. But afterwards, few remembered what he had said or even the general outline of his message.[14]

Between 1904 and 1908 he enrolled as a special student in the Kirksville State Normal School, but he seldom remained in residence for more than a quarter at a time. Though he had little opportunity for concentrated study, he easily earned high grades. He took basic work in chemistry, English, psychology, and physical education, but his real interests were in history and Latin. He studied ancient, medieval, and modern history and read Ovid, Caesar, and Cicero.[15] The pressure of his evangelical work and his need to support himself while in college kept him out of many student activities. Nevertheless, he found time to serve as class curator, to participate in intercollegiate debates, and to represent his school at a Young Men's Christian Association conference. Faculty members thought that he had a bright future.

His fellow students liked him, although they made fun of his most obvious asset—his "ceaseless flow of big words and hot air."[16]

As his reputation as an orator spread, Frank found his services in demand on the sawdust circuit as a "soul tamer." In the summers of 1907 and 1908 he and some other young clergymen urged perspiring crowds to heed the slogan emblazoned on the sagging top of their shabby canvas tent: Go WITH GOD. Handsome and neatly dressed in a white linen suit, a dark tie, a broad-brimmed straw hat, and a pair of sporty shoes, Frank became a familiar figure on the evangelical circuits of northern Missouri and southern Iowa.[17] During these summer tours he came to the attention of William "Billy" Sunday, who in the summer of 1909 hired him as an assistant for a summer-long crusade against sin and corruption in Marshalltown, Iowa. His association with Sunday left a deep impression on Frank. "I saw the inside of the mind and the heart of the man in those six weeks, and, as a result, I never shared the judgment of him expressed by the cynical and sophisticated," he later recounted. "I watched him indulge in gyrations and grimaces, even in prayer, that shook my sense of fitness, but I rarely found men leaving his clapboarded tabernacles after such performances with lessened reverence for God and decency and rightness in their lives."[18]

His summer with Billy Sunday's evangelical crusade was a rewarding one for Glenn Frank. He earned money to further his education and became well known to the sinners of the little Iowa town, who nodded sagely and pronounced him a great success. More importantly, he learned much by observing Sunday's techniques, particularly his style of public speaking and the publicity by which he sold both redemption and himself to the farmers and shopkeepers of Marshalltown. Frank's sojourn on the revival circuit was, in effect, to serve as his apprenticeship in successive careers as journalist, educator, and politician. To be sure, question marks remained.

Did he want to remain a part of the Missouri scene? Was his success as an evangelist merely a consequence of pride and ambition rather than a true calling? But by the autumn of 1909 at least one thing was clear: there was no longer any question about whether Glenn Frank would succeed, but only about how great his success would be.

II

The Evanston Years

IN THE FALL OF 1909, Glenn Frank left Missouri. He went to Evanston, Illinois—the farthest away from home he had ever been—to enroll in Northwestern University. Initially, his admission appeared doubtful. When the registrar suspiciously questioned the academic standing of the Kirksville State Normal School, Frank took his case directly to a dean. He forthrightly told how he had preached the faith of the Wesleys as a circuit rider, how he had done so with the single purpose in mind of attending Northwestern, and how he had read "hundreds of books" to compensate for the poor quality of instruction he had received in Kirksville. He emphasized that he had served as an assistant to Billy Sunday, whose tirades against Demon Rum found favor with Methodists throughout the nation and especially in Evanston, the national headquarters of the Women's Christian Temperance Union. The dean intervened and secured his admission to Northwestern with sophomore standing. Later, Frank jokingly claimed that he had "sort of cheated his way in."[1]

At the time that he registered, the university administration was transforming Northwestern from a religiously oriented co-educational liberal arts college, designed primarily to train ministers and to indoctrinate middle-class boys and girls with Methodist tenets, into a major institution of higher learning, devoted particularly to scholarship and research. Northwestern already boasted separate schools of law, oratory, music, medicine, and divinity, as well as a post-graduate program. Although the university retained its Methodist ties, a secular tone increasingly prevailed. Aside from the divinity school, most faculty members were laymen with graduate training. Many of the younger instructors sympathized with the growing emphasis on the social sciences in the United States and were aware of the scientific canons of German scholarship. Most of Northwestern's thousand students came from the Chicago area; their fathers were usually professional or businessmen.[2] It would be hard to envisage an environment more different from the one Frank had known.

The ambitious former circuit rider intrigued his classmates. At an age when for many students life had not yet begun to take on too serious an aspect, Glenn Frank stood out above his fellows as one who combined a youthful zest for life with a sophistication born not of urban experience but of the earnest business of rural evangelism. Both his capacity for self-expression and the magnetism of his personality distinguished him from the rank-and-file. One of his contemporaries recalled that "while he apparently wasn't more than a year or two older than most of us, his background of experience led us to consider him as a quite unusual person, and one of such a serious mind that we weren't sure how he would fit into the college scheme of things . . . . " Frank quickly dispelled these doubts by showing a ready ability to adapt to the new environment. After the first shock of discovering his "sky pilot" background, his classmates came to admire his intellectual capacity and cultural interests. For many, he became a delightful companion. He was voted the senior who did the most to further the interests of the university and the best-looking man in his class.[3]

Frank participated in a large number of extracurricular activities, and he soon became a familiar campus figure. He joined Delta Tau Delta fraternity because, he claimed, "I was short of money, and I found that I could run a boarding bill larger in a fraternity than in a boarding house." He served on the inter-fraternity council; he joined the staff of the *Northwestern Magazine,* a literary publication; he helped prepare the college yearbook; he became a member of the Aleph Teth Nun debating society; he participated in campus politics; he attended meetings of the Oxford Club, an association of divinity students; and he acted in dramatic productions.[4] The apex of his theatrical experience came when he played the lead in a comedy called *The Father of the Boys.* With characteristic collegiate enthusiasm the reviewer for the school newspaper wrote, "The father of the boys was played with great dignity by Glenn Frank. This is no doubt the heaviest part of the play, but it was taken care of in good shape. The father is a very conservative person at first, but later he throws off his provincialism and shows the boys he, too, can be a leader of the smart set."[5] Frank probably had little difficulty getting into the spirit of the part, for in some sense this was the role he was unconsciously to play in real life.

In his senior year Frank edited the *Northwestern Magazine,* a task which he said required "a large range of intellect, varied acquirements, and great strength of character." He somewhat pompously announced in the journal that his purpose was to promote "justice, audacity with fidelity, and omniscience with truthfulness." Exhibiting a flair for editing and promotion, he changed the format and broadened the scope of the previously moribund monthly. Besides printing the usual contributions from students, he published interviews—including an eyewitness account of the sinking of the *Titanic*—added illustrations to enliven the pages, and persuaded alumni and faculty to contribute articles. He also worked vigorously to attract advertising and encouraged his readers to patronize the magazine's advertisers. "A merchant advertises in a school publication," he informed his readers, "for one or more of these three reasons: CHARITY–RECIPROCITY–OPPORTUNITY. If he advertises and receives no return it is CHARITY. If he enjoys your patronage whether he advertises or not, it is RECIPROCITY. But if you read his advertisements and are persuaded to visit his store, to examine his line of goods, it is OPPORTUNITY. The advertising pages of this magazine are here for a purpose—skip them and they become CHARITY—read them and they create OPPORTUNITY."⁶ Many of his readers followed his advice. On the whole, it was widely believed that Frank had "wrought well" and that he produced "one of the best college publications . . . to be found among American Colleges and Universities."⁷ Frank's capacity for huckstering appeared very early, reflecting an affinity for promotion that was to stand him in good stead for the rest of his career.

Frank devoted his leading feature in each issue of the *Northwestern* to an essay about an author whom he considered to have influenced modern life. With sophomoric enthusiasm he evaluated the character and personality of Robert Louis Stevenson, Theodore Roosevelt, Count Leo Tolstoy, Henrik Ibsen, Edmond Rostand, George Bernard Shaw, Maurice Maeterlinck, and G. K. Chesterton. Each, he sagely announced, had developed a philsophy of life worthy of incarnation. Stevenson, whose complete works he claimed to have read "seven times repeated," was a combination "optimist, moralist, stylist, toiler, iconoclast, psychologist"; Shaw was "a prince of cocksureness"; Rostand either a "genius, aesthete, egomaniac, or procureur"; Ibsen "an agitator in literature"; and Maeterlinck "a Belgian mystic." Chesterton represented "the desire of the Age of Doubt for the satisfaction and peace of an Age of Hate," while Tolstoy's system of ethics seemed impracticable. According to Frank, Theodore Roosevelt spoke to the man who wanted to serve his generation and imposed upon him the duty to develop "an efficient selfhood," which would then be sacrificed for "the sake of others."⁸ Most of his readers thought that his observations were pungent and insightful. When Frank's editorial tenure ended, his awed successor quavered that "it is hard for the ordinary mortal to follow in the footsteps of a genius."⁹

Throughout his college years Frank also capitalized on his talents as a platform orator. He began to take private lessons in the Northwestern School of Oratory, but the teachers soon admitted that he knew more than they did about the art of public speaking. A contemporary claimed that he probably looked upon lecturing as a "racket."[10] But Frank realized that he had a gift for words, and he shrewdly made the most of his talents to defray some of his college expenses. His skilled delivery and clever use of figures of speech allowed him to appear as an authority on many unfamiliar subjects and frequently compensated for lack of content. He lectured extensively throughout the Evanston area, usually before religious groups, emphasizing his theme that religion had "more to do with the streets than with the stars; more to do with the grimy hands of labor than with the golden harps of angels." Frank contended that a strong religious belief helped man to live morally and justly; the future would then take care of itself. "The test of religion is to make bad men good and to make good men better," he declared. "The master of the world has a plan into which every man can fit."[11] His listeners, most of whom were educated people imbued with the religious modernism of the period, found his approach appealing.

Frank also used his declamatory talents for secular purposes. On two occasions he won major oratorical contests. During his senior year he won the local Kirk Prize with a well-constructed oration, then carried the school colors to the prestigious Northern Oratorical Contest, where he vanquished contestants from other midwestern universities. In a speech entitled "Morals and Machinery, or a Public Age with a Private Conscience," Frank argued that the realities of an industrial America necessitated the development of a new set of social values. Stressing what was later to become one of his favorite themes, he capitalized on the current Progressive ferment and generalized about his subject without alienating either audience or judges. "May the ethical and educational leaders in our nation," he urged, "teach so clearly and plead so passionately that some day we will feel that the man who refuses to protect adequately his workingmen is as much a murderer, when needless loss of life occurs, as was the primitive man when he beat out his brother's brains with a war club; that the man who takes advantage of the poor man's economic need to hold him in industrial slavery is as morally culpable as the man who cracked a whip over a slave's bare back; that the man who pays such insufficient wages to his shop girls that they are forced into the vice districts to supplement their earnings is a violator of the womanhood of America. . . . America cannot keep herself clean with a private conscience. We must grow a social conscience that will produce a public morality or we will pass into the cemetery of dead civilizations." Listeners said that Frank's colorful metaphors lent force and direction to his "masterful production."[12]

Glenn Frank increasingly came to savor an audience's hushed silence and its climactic roar of approval. But he was never a man to rest on his laurels. Driven by ego and by financial necessity, he spent his college vacations on the midwestern Chautauqua and Lyceum circuits. There he came into contact with people who hungered not for the emotional release of evangelical brimstone but for a vision of a wider world—a world of books and ideas, of faraway peoples and places, and of the promise of a better life here and now. Advance publicity heralded him as a combination lecturer, minister, college man, and student of books and affairs, a veritable "Dynamo of Energy" whose pleasing voice, sincere manner, and outgoing personality instantly won over his audiences. Frank based his lectures on the assumption "that the crowd was hungry for straight-from-the-shoulder treatment of the serious problems of our Industrial and Ethical life." Behaving for all the world like a character out of Sinclair Lewis, he hawked his spellbinding rhetoric along the Main Streets of the Midwest. He earned extra money by acting as manager of the unit he accompanied, looking after the condition of the tent, directing the crew, supervising the arrangement of the platform, introducing his associates, and counting the gate receipts.[13]

Frank regaled the crowds along the circuit with lectures

which he said bristled with a mixture of "red blooded earnestness" and "fight and aggressiveness." He discoursed engagingly on the patriots of the century, the making of a scholar, the search for certainty, the role of the Negro in a democracy, the crisis points in society, and literature in modern life—the latter a summary of the articles he had written for the *Northwestern Magazine*. His most popular series consisted of five addresses on the relationship of the individual to the Bible, to the Church, and to the Saints, with speculations on whether people should "get into" or "run away" from the world. Wherever he appeared, he gave a good account of himself. An editor in Huron, South Dakota, noted that "his work won a large place in the esteem of the people" because "they are put in such a popular form that the man on the street thoroughly enjoys them." In Hamilton, Missouri, he drew larger audiences than a former governor of the state and was the center of attention on the Chautauqua grounds.[14] Huron and Hamilton were not, it was true, New York or Boston, but they represented a start, and the financial returns from his lectures—more than a thousand dollars a summer—far exceeded the stipend of a Missouri circuit rider.

In spite of his crowded speaking schedule on and off the Northwestern campus, Frank somehow found time to attend classes. He broadened his intellectual horizons by majoring in classical history and sharpened his awareness of contemporary problems by studying economic theory. In retrospect—like so many undergraduates before and since—he fretted about the compartmentalization of his courses: "At 9 o'clock in the morning I studied fourth century history; at 10 o'clock, 19th century economy; at 11 o'clock, 14th century literature. Hour by hour I emigrated from one to another of three perfectly airtight worlds." Even so, he applied himself diligently, keeping detailed and well-organized notes, which he bound into black notebooks for future use. His grades were above average, though not conspicuously so. During a typical semester he received two A's, a B, and a C.[15] Two of his former teachers, Walter Dill Scott and James Alton James, later recalled that he had demonstrated a ready grasp of basic problems and concepts. Scott thought him "the most brilliant mind that I had come in contact with among undergraduates." According to Professor James, Frank "devoured" the writings of Frederick Jackson Turner, agreeing with the historian of the American frontier that a new social order made individualism an outmoded concept. By his junior year, James said, Frank gave evidence of an alert, vigorous intellect.[16]

Abram Harris, president of Northwestern, watched Frank's progress with growing interest. He believed that Frank possessed the attributes—aggressiveness, organizational skill, self-confidence, speaking ability, and a background in the Methodist ministry—which the university was seeking in its alumni secretary, a newly created post. During Frank's senior year, in December, 1911, Harris offered him the position, to take effect the following autumn. Frank, who was still rather half-heartedly planning to go on to divinity school, quickly accepted. "I closed matters with President Harris on Saturday," he told his parents. "I guess I'll be secretary of Northwestern University next year. The salary is not big but good and the opportunity is very great. I will get $1200 and expenses and will have my summers for Chautauqua work and a month for lecturing in the winter. . . . Don't you think I'm wise in taking it?"[17]

Frank graduated in June, 1912, after delivering a commencement oration on "The Heresy of Silence," and following a summer of lecturing he assumed his new duties as alumni secretary. Announcing his appointment, President Harris emphasized the university's desire for improved alumni relations through the establishment of a clearinghouse for information and the organization of additional Northwestern clubs throughout the country.[18] Privately, he told Frank that he hoped the alumni office would attract more students to Northwestern by working closely with Methodist ministers, and that it would raise sufficient money to finance the alumni program. Warning Frank that he would have to depend largely upon his own judgment and initiative, Harris counseled him to maintain his interest in religious and intellectual affairs, and to reflect carefully on each phase of the new program. Finally, sensing Frank's proclivity for flamboyant salesmanship, Harris cautioned him to "keep within the strictest bounds of good taste so as to avoid 'blowing our own horn.' "[19]

During the next three years, Frank worked enthusiastically and effectively on the university's behalf. He revolutionized the traditional concept of alumni relations. He doubled the endowment fund, recruited more students, and revealed a distinct administrative talent. In the process, he broadened the scope of his responsibilities beyond the point which Harris had envisioned. He played a role in the financing of new dormitories, organized an annual alumni night, edited an alumni magazine, and stimulated the formation of a galaxy of alumni organizations. "If there is no Northwestern Club in your city," he wrote in the *Alumni Journal*, "and you do not know who are the Northwestern graduates living there, write the Alumni Secretary for a list. . . . Obey the impulse!"[20]

Frank spent most of his time on the road. Adhering to what he termed a "staggering schedule," he traveled throughout the Midwest and occasionally as far east as New York and as far west as Denver. In a three-year period he addressed more than 20,000 high school pupils on "general educational subjects." During two months in 1913, he visited twenty-two cities, in five states, often making several appearances in a single day. At Topeka, Kansas, for example, his schedule began at 9 A.M. with an address at the Washburn University Law School and ended with an evening banquet, three speeches and an alumni luncheon later.

"Everywhere," Frank remarked, "the eager interest, the loyalty, and the unfailing courtesy of the graduates . . . made the work a delight." Indeed, the very success of his campaign so burdened the alumni office with additional demands on its services that Frank had repeatedly to urge Northwestern graduates to volunteer their services and to assume greater responsibility for operating local alumni groups.[21]

Glenn Frank, now in his early twenties, seemed to be achieving the success which his friends and neighbors in

Green Top had predicted for him. For the first time in his life he had money in his pocket. To be sure, as alumni secretary he was obliged to dress and to live far more grandly than before. But his income from the university, combined with his lecture fees, was more than adequate to the demands imposed upon him, and within a short time he had saved enough to contribute substantially to the support of his aging parents. He built them a house on a piece of land he bought for them in Green Top, and he volunteered to pay the taxes on the property, enabling them to live out their lives rent-free.[22] Nevertheless, in more ways than one, Frank had severed his ties with the past. Step by step, his career was bearing him further and further away from all that Green Top represented.

More than anything else, it was the lecture circuit which was shifting the direction of his life and accentuating the thrust of his personality. In his own mind, his private speaking engagements created no conflict of interest with his function as alumni secretary, for he believed, as did President Harris of Northwestern, that his widening reputation on the lecture circuit served to enhance the university's prestige and to strengthen its bonds with its alumni. At the same time, Frank was not unmindful of the many benefits which he derived personally, not the least of which was money. As an impressionable young man with a rural background and limited financial resources, he tended to measure success in material terms, the more so as his contacts with well-to-do society increased. Inevitably, Frank took on some of the polished, sophisticated urbanity of the larger metropolitan centers he visited. His association with Northwestern soon carried him from the dusty, sweltering tents of the Chautauqua circuit to the auditoriums, theaters, and gilded dining rooms of Boston, New York, and Philadelphia. No less inevitably, and doubtless unconsciously, he began to tailor his rhetoric to the tastes of the business community. Religious themes and allusions, though never absent from his addresses, occupied a declining place of order. The brimstone of the evangelical circuit gave way to a bland, more palatable message—a message which evoked a sympathetic response among merchants, manufacturers, and brokers. Unknowingly, Frank was making the transition from boy evangelist to spokesman for a business-oriented Social Gospel. Just as unknowingly, he was anticipating the intellectual climate of the age of Harding.

III

The Boston Years

GLENN FRANK NOW STOOD at one of many successive crossroads in his life. In retrospect, he seemed always to have been at the right place at precisely the right moment. In 1909, after less than six years of experience as a preacher an itinerant evangelist, he had been noticed by Billy Sunday, and in the summer of concentrated experience which followed he not only polished his inherent oratorical skills but seemed also to have found his vocation. His decision to seek admission to Northwestern, however, represented more than a determination to enter the ministry; it represented a break with his limited rural horizons. It seemed unlikely that a college and divinity school graduate would ever again be content to minister to the Possums and Green Tops of the Midwest. Frank's successes as collegiate actor, editor, and platform orator convinced him—if indeed he needed convincing—that there were few goals that he was not equipped to attain, and that a secular career could be as satisfying as one in the Methodist church. Thus, when President Harris began his search for someone to organize and manage Northwestern's alumni office, Glenn Frank was not only an obvious candidate, but, with his waning enthusiasm for a career in the ministry, an available one.

In accepting the secretaryship, Frank did not commit himself to Northwestern University for life. He was determined to devote all his energies to the new position, but at the same time he was no less determined to make the most of the opportunities which came his way. Over the next three years his growing affluence, his emerging urbanity, and his widening circle of personal contacts assured him that the secretaryship presaged other, more responsible positions both within and without the university. Indeed, after only twenty months in the service of Northwestern, he was seriously considered for the presidency of the University of West Virginia. Frank was briefly tempted, but once having found metropolitan life to his taste, he felt little desire to return to a locale reminiscent of his childhood.

In December, 1915, Glenn Frank was recommended by Walter Dill Scott for a position as private secretary to Edward A. Filene, the eminent Boston merchant-philanthropist. Several reasons underlay his decision to leave Northwestern. Above all it was Boston, which symbolized to Frank the true American heritage—the cultivated literary world, the mannered social order, the old houses and the old wealth. Scarcely less important was the attraction of associating with Filene himself, who in his approach to business, management, and philanthropy epitomized Frank's image of the enlightened, socially conscious progressive. Finally, there was the salary of $7,500 a year, a substantial increase over his Northwestern salary and expenses.

Frank quickly settled down in Boston, renting a small apartment close enough to walk to his office in the Filene Building on Washington Street. From the start, Frank was captivated and stimulated by Edward Filene's far-ranging business and intellectual interests. Fifty-five years old in 1915, Filene had spent the preceding quarter-century actively managing the department store which he and his brother Lincoln had taken over from their father William Filene in 1890. William, a Jewish ribbon merchant, had emigrated from the Prussian town of Poznan in 1848 and had first established a dry goods store in New York City. When that venture failed following the Civil War, William moved to Salem, Massachusetts, where he again entered the dry goods industry. Successful in this second attempt, he eventually established other stores in nearby Lynn and also at Bath, Maine.

In the late 1870's, William decided to consolidate his businesses and to move to Boston. He established himself on Winter Street, two blocks from Boston Common, in a one-room store, which, though small, achieved a modest air of elegance from its "genuine marble floor" and attractively appointed windows. With the assistance of two of his sons, Edward and Lincoln, the elder Filene rapidly expanded the enterprise and by 1890, when he retired, the firm occupied a five-story building around the corner on Washington Street.

The very success of the Filene enterprise, however, exacted a toll from the family. It ruined William's health and stood in the way of a college education for the sons. Edward, for example, born in Salem in 1860 and educated both in Germany and Massachusetts, aspired to enter Harvard College. Contrary to the predictions of his family, he passed the entrance examination in 1879, but the collapse of his father's health and the burgeoning demands of the department store forced him to abandon his plans for a college education.

Edward Filene quickly reconciled himself to this disappointment and concentrated his energies on managing William Filene, Sons and Company. Within a decade he and his brother Lincoln assumed complete control of the firm and rapidly built it into a multi-million-dollar Boston institution and one of the largest department stores in the country. By nature an innovator, Edward Filene was always alert to new modes of promotion and mass distribution. He pioneered the "automatic bargain basement," a radical system of retailing designed to move the largest possible volume of goods in the shortest possible time. William Filene's, Sons and Company achieved this by date-stamping its merchandise and progressively reducing the price over a thirty-day period, at which time all unsold goods were donated to charity.[1]

Yet for all his business success, Edward Filene was not obsessed with moneymaking. On the contrary, even before the construction of a huge emporium on the corner of

Washington and Winter streets in 1913 and his gradual withdrawal from the active management of the firm, the introspective Filene had increasingly interested himself in a wide variety of social and economic questions. Deeply influenced by the intellectual currents of the time and familiar with the writings of American, English, and German reformers, he felt it his duty to devote some of his time, energy, and resources to what were then commonly termed "works of social betterment."

Being a practical man, he tackled the problems closest at hand, and turned his store into a showplace for the practical application of current social and economic theories. He inaugurated a profit-sharing plan, granted his employees voting representation at board meetings, formed an employees' arbitration committee to settle labor disputes and cases of misconduct, and established a co-operative association to conduct social work and maintain a company hospital. Ideally, he hoped that one day his employees would assume joint ownership of the firm.

On balance, however, Filene largely failed to derive the anticipated satisfaction from these experiments in what he called "business democracy." To his chagrin, he discovered that his enlightened policies only served to whet the appetites of his employees for even greater concessions. In particular, they demanded higher wages and shorter hours, and the arbitration committee seemed to encourage dissension rather than corporate harmony. Filene soon retreated from his earlier idealism, discontinuing many of his projects in "business democracy" and abandoning his long-range goal of joint ownership. Leaving the day-to-day management of the store to subordinates, he devoted himself to broader philanthropic projects, to the Peace Movement, and to economic reform.

Gradually Filene emerged as an economic statesman—a prophet and apostle of a new economic era. He preached a gospel of mass production, mass purchasing power, and mass consumption, using as his text his own successes in large-scale merchandising. To all who would listen to him—

chambers of commerce, service clubs, national and international businessmen's conventions—he expounded his message: Capitalism could survive the radicals which threatened to destroy it only by adopting his doctrine of "enlightened selfishness."

Shortly after the turn of the century, Filene turned his interest especially to ways of providing the poorer members of society with credit in times of emergency. He had noted that many of his own workers had failed to make adequate provision for hard times—illness and unemployment, for example—and that they were often forced to pay exorbitant rates of interest. During a world tour in 1907, Filene found what he thought was a solution to this problem in the credit-union system which the British had set up in India as an alternative to the village money lenders. Soon after his return to Massachusetts he began to campaign for legislation authorizing the organization of credit unions, and in 1909 the General Court passed the first such American law. Once established, the credit-union movement rapidly expanded, and other states soon followed the Massachusetts example.

Filene also became deeply interested in the prevention of war. Appalled by the holocaust in Europe, he became a devoted supporter of the League to Enforce Peace, and especially its objective of an international organization dedicated to preserving the peace. His activities on behalf of the Peace Movement brought Filene widespread recognition and decorations from several foreign governments.[2]

However, many critics questioned Filene's motives. Despite his contributions to American business, including the organization of the national Chamber of Commerce, and his philanthropic activities, he was charged on the one hand with using his great wealth to exculpate the Robber Barons, and on the other hand with seeking to dominate the charitable and other organizations to which he contributed. Associates thought him haughty and overbearing, though they readily admitted that he demanded as much of himself as he did of others. No one was indifferent to Filene; he was a man "with whom one could get along perfectly or not at all."[3]

By 1915 Edward Filene was involved in so many causes, many of them controversial, that he felt the need for an assistant who could not only relieve him of some of the pressures on his time but could also help to assuage his critics. Glenn Frank was well suited to such a role. His college background and his experience as alumni secretary allowed him to move confidently in the Filene circle. His experience on the lecture circuit and as the editor of two successful Northwestern publications fitted him in other ways for the role which the Boston merchant envisaged for his assistant. As President Harris had said, Frank had the leadership qualities, the analytical mind, and the personal magnetism to succeed in the business world.[4]

Frank found that Filene set a driving pace. He had barely reached Boston when he and his new employer set off on a grueling trip to California and a demanding schedule of conferences, lectures, and meetings. But Frank was used to travel and adjusted smoothly. Indeed, he quickly won Filene's confidence and fulfilled the promise which his admirers at Northwestern had predicted, and within a year Filene had made him more than a mere administrative assistant. Rather, Frank became Filene's confidant, speechwriter, private secretary, and personal representative—in short, his alter ego.

Filene's principal interest at this time was the League to Enforce Peace, to which he had subscribed $25,000. Frank always accompanied Filene on his trips to the League's New York headquarters, and represented his employer when other commitments prevented his attendance. With the entrance of the United States into the war in 1917, Frank devoted almost all of his working time to the peace effort. Filene had him help mount a massive propaganda campaign designed to convince grassroots America that military victory would have meaning only if the Allies were prepared to guarantee the peace. As the most powerful of the pacifist organizations, the League to Enforce Peace did more than any other organization to win President Woodrow Wilson's support for a league of nations. And exhausting though the work was, Frank found it exhilarating. As Filene's agent, he came to know the luminaries of the League's inner circles—Abbott Lawrence Lowell, president of Harvard University; Hamilton Holt, crusading editor of *The Independent;* Jane Addams, founder of Hull House; and William Howard Taft, titular head of the League to Enforce Peace.[5]

Frank relished these contacts, the more so since the great and near-great seemed to be impressed with his capabilities. "President Taft and others were in my room at a meeting this afternoon," he wrote. "We have had a great time and concluded a big deal I've been working on all week." He left this conference with soaring spirits, convinced that the former President of the United States had "taken a very gratifying liking" to him.[6]

Frank's rising stock as Filene's aide-de-camp and publicist was paralleled by his emergence as an author in his own right. His first important literary effort was *The Stakes of the War,* which he wrote in 1918 in collaboration with Lothrop Stoddard, a Harvard Ph.D. with an independent income. The authors argued that in their own interest the American people must learn the political, strategic, racial, cultural, and economic factors which demanded solution at the peace table. Frank and Stoddard documented their contention with detailed information about the characteristics of each nation involved in hostilities. "Foreign affairs have become the personal concern of the man in the street, no less than the professional concern of the scholar and the trader," they wrote. "Not that these facts have not always had profound influence among some Americans and upon American interests, but it remained for the war to force upon us, as a people, a belated recognition of the fact that we are part and parcel of a world of interlaced interests in which no nation can play a lone hand."

The book, published by the Century Company of New

York, received routine notices which indicated that it had value as a reference work. Frank, described on the title page as a "Sometime Lecturer on Social-Economics," made certain that it came to the attention of people in high places. Under Filene's signature, he sent dozens of copies to various business leaders and government officials. In return he received only brief acknowledgements. But the book sold extremely well. During the first year of its publication Frank made $1,291.48 in royalties.

Although Frank and Stoddard had planned a series of books dealing with contemporary issues, Frank withdrew from the partnership following the publication in 1920 of Stoddard's *The Rising Tide of Color,* a racist tract prophesying the doom of Nordic civilization unless the Anglo-Saxon and other northern European races combined against the threat of "racially inferior stock." From principle rather than from expediency, Frank hastily disassociated himself from Stoddard's extremist views.[7]

Even before the appearance of *The Rising Tide of Color,* Frank had shown himself capable of standing alone as an author. His *Politics of Industry,* on which he had been working for several years and which appeared in 1919, represented an effort to systematize his thinking on labor-management questions. Drawing heavily upon the writings of social scientists and economists, and particularly upon the speeches and writings of Edward A. Filene, Frank contended that America stood at a crossroads. Unless the United States could make the transition from war to peace, the rash of strikes already plaguing the industrial economy would become a chronic rather than a temporary condition. What was needed, he contended, was responsible leadership. And he deplored the lack of foresight shown by labor, management, and government. In Frank's view, trade-union leaders seemed unable to press for higher wages and improve working conditions without disrupting production. Employers, in turn, continued to rely upon discredited methods for dealing with labor's demands—resorting to strikebreakers, private police forces, and, in extreme cases, the militia. Governmental efforts to solve these problems were equally misguided, and *ad hoc* legislation treated the symptoms, not the cause, of industrial conflict.

Frank implored industrial leaders to take the initiative, and to tackle social unrest at its roots by instituting a system of industrial councils at which the representatives of both labor and management could fashion harmonious and democratic solutions. Such councils, Frank believed, would promote industrial peace by practicing "the social virtues of efficiency, justice, and sanity. . . . "[8] These modest recommendations appealed to the captains of business and industry, who had long since wearied of the strident criticism of dissident reformers. When more fully developed over the next ten years, these ideas would enlarge Frank's reputation as a spokesman for enlightened capitalism.

Throughout his Evanston and Boston years, Glenn Frank formed no deep, personal friendships. It was not for lack of opportunity, for he was constantly on the go, moving effortlessly within a dozen overlapping circles of acquaintances. He dazzled most of the people whom he met, but he was seemingly a man whom everyone liked but no one loved. To this generalization, however, there was one exception.

During his youth in Green Top he had become attached to Mary Smith, the daughter of a prosperous hardware merchant in Glenwood, Missouri. The young couple had spoken vaguely of the future, and it was widely expected in the area that they would one day marry. But when Frank had gone to Northwestern and Mary to Stephens College, a fashionable finishing school in Columbia, their paths had seemed to diverge, and Frank especially had seemed bent on severing all his Missouri ties. However, they had kept their friendship alive through correspondence, and increasingly Frank began to share his hopes, ambitions, and innermost thoughts with the girl. Mary was able to see Frank only on his infrequent visits to Missouri, but she provided him with as much affection and understanding as he seemed to desire. In addition, as she identified herself with the aspirations of the rising young alumni secretary, her own latent ambition asserted itself. At first glance the suave, urbane Glenn Frank and the rather plain, untraveled Mary Smith seemed unsuited to each other. But she came from a respected, well-to-do family; she held a college degree in an age when most women did not; she showed every promise of acquiring the requisite social graces; and, what is more, she shared Frank's ambition to get on in life.

Once established in Boston, Frank began to court Mary in earnest. "I have pictured you in every chair and at every moment of the day," he wrote in one of his many letters. "It's good to have a vivid imagination. I don't know how I would get along if I didn't."[9] Mary responded warmly. Her father heartily approved of his future son-in-law, and later remarked that Glenn was all he had hoped for—"a good clean nice man [and] a credit to all."[10]

Glenn Frank and Mary Smith were married at Bofinger Memorial Church in St. Louis at 11:00 A.M. on Saturday, June 2, 1917, by the Right Rev. Daniel S. Tuttle, presiding bishop of the Episcopal Church in America and a life-long friend of the bride's family. Mary, gowned in a traveling costume of dark blue, worn with "a chic little hat," was attended by her sister as maid of honor, and was given away by her father. A friend of Glenn's from Chicago acted as best man. A wedding breakfast at the home of the father of the bride followed the ceremony.

After a brief honeymoon, the couple made their first home together at 496 Commonwealth Avenue in Boston, an address quite in keeping with the aspirations of the newly married Franks. There they entertained modestly but frequently, and their relatives, friends, and acquaintances alike remarked about the refined and harmonious atmosphere of the Frank household. They also noted the astonishing degree to which the two complemented each other. The birth of a son, Glenn, Jr., on December 7, 1918, added still further to their happiness.[11]

Yet happy though the Franks were in Boston, they never fully identified with the city, and seemed to regard it merely as a way station in their lives. To be sure, all the wealth, breeding, and monuments to the past were there, as Frank had expected; but, as always, a newcomer—whether from Ireland, Italy, or Missouri—found that an old and aristocratic society presented many closed doors. Frank did meet President Lowell of Harvard and other important Bostonians in his philanthropic work, and especially in his role as Filene's emissary to the League to Enforce Peace. But such acquaintanceships never ripened into friendship, nor did they give Frank and his wife entree into Boston society. The problem, of course, was that Filene himself could open few doors. Though widely respected for his good works and his business acumen, as far as Boston was concerned Filene could never rise above his Jewish immigrant's background. By force of circumstances, then, Frank found himself drawn to the coterie of politicians, reformers, and intellectuals of New York City, where ability accounted for more and ancestry for less.

By 1919, Glenn Frank felt that he had accomplished, both for Filene and for himself, all that it was possible to achieve in Boston. The end of the war and America's subsequent rejection of the League of Nations also spelled the gradual demise of the League to Enforce Peace, and soon transformed a stimulating job into a dreary and routine one. Nor was Frank unmindful of the fact that working for Filene was like walking a tightrope. Filene's reputation for impulsively dismissing his executives was well known, and the attrition rate among his personal assistants was inordinately high. So far, Frank had succeeded admirably as Filene's secretary; prudence suggested that he seek another avenue of advancement while he still retained the merchant's esteem and good will.[12] So when he learned that the *Century Magazine* in New York needed a new associate editor, he decided to investigate the opportunity.

IV

The Century Magazine

A NATIONALLY DISTRIBUTED literary maga-
zine, the *Century* had originally been called *Scribner's* and
had been published since 1881 by the Century Company, one
of America's greatest publishing houses. It reached its zenith
under the editorship of Richard Watson Gilder, and in the
late 1880's had a circulation of more than 200,000 and earned
a large income from its heavy volume of advertising. At
that time it had a reputation as one of the most prestigious
magazines in America. A long series of articles on the Civil
War as seen and interpreted by participants in the conflict,
later republished in four volumes as *Battles and Leaders,*
appealed to readers and critics, as did fiction by such glittering lights as Bret Harte, Mark Twain, and William Dean
Howells.

However, the advent of mass circulation magazines such
as *McClure's* and *Collier's* had hurt the *Century* by increasing the competition for authors, readers, and advertisers.
Gilder was slow to adjust to the times, and continued to publish what the trade called a "quality" magazine, preferring
this dignified approach to the muckraking sensationalism
introduced by his competitors. When he died in 1905 the
Century was in financial difficulties. Successive changes in
editorial policy failed to halt a steady decline in circulation,
and by the end of the First World War it had only 50,000 subscribers. Nevertheless, the president of the Century Com-

pany, W. Morgan Schuster, was determined to continue publication if he could do so without pouring in a vast amount of new capital.[1]

Frank learned of the associate editorship through a friend, a former Illinois newspaper editor turned motion-picture producer, Benjamin Hampton, who was also a friend of Schuster's. Despite the waning fortunes of the *Century,* Frank was immediately attracted to the position because of the magazine's continuing reputation as an influential American publication. The task of restoring the magazine to its former pre-eminence presented both an opportunity and a challenge—considerations which meant much to Frank at this stage in his career. His immediate problem was to convince Schuster that he was the right man for the position.

In April of 1919, Frank went to New York to seek the counsel of Hampton, who told him that Schuster was then heavily involved in other affairs and advised him to delay asking for an interview for a week or two. Hampton expressed confidence in Frank's ability, but advised him to "work out a real plan to sell [himself] to Schuster."[2] Rather than returning to Boston, Frank remained in New York drafting his proposals and waiting for the auspicious moment to approach the publisher. When the two finally met, Schuster was sufficiently impressed with Frank to conclude the preliminary arrangements on the spot.

Under the terms of employment, Schuster agreed to place Frank's name on the masthead of the magazine as associate editor, left him free to come and go as he pleased, and set his salary at $7,500 per year. In addition to giving general editorial direction to the magazine, Frank was required to write sixteen pages of copy on topics of his own choosing for each month's issue. Frank hesitated before agreeing to what he felt was a heavy writing schedule. "I think it is bad editorial policy to have one man write so much," he wrote to his wife, "but you can't expect to get everything perfect to start with."[3] The position as Schuster outlined it, however, possessed advantages which more than compensated for these editorial demands. Schuster was well aware of

Frank's talents as a public lecturer, and encouraged him to continue his speaking engagements across the country. "The more reputation you can gain for yourself and the more contacts you can establish, the better for the Century Co.," Schuster told him. This arrangement delighted Frank: he knew that he could earn an additional net income of about ten thousand dollars from his fifty to sixty lectures per year.

Frank plunged into the editorship with characteristic zeal. Within a few months he felt assured enough to offer Schuster detailed recommendations for the revamping of the *Century*. The problems of publishing, he told his employer, were similar to those of investing: "The man wins who comes nearest to seeing what the demands will be so many months or years ahead—and prepares for it." Above all, a good editor had to know his readers and their tastes. Frank, who had learned a great deal about publishing from Hamilton Holt, whose *Independent* was also losing subscribers, suggested that the *Century* abandon its traditional format—a hodgepodge of literary pieces and public-affairs articles. Frank observed that he regularly purchased the *Literary Digest*, the *New Republic*, the *Review of Reviews*, and the *Saturday Evening Post* without inspecting their contents, secure in the knowledge that they would contain the reading fare which he anticipated. He bought other journals only because particular issues contained articles or features of special interest. The *Century*, he argued, should also be tailored to a particular audience—an audience which would soon come to expect each number of the magazine to touch upon a set range of contemporary issues and to package them in a neat, predictable format. But not all of the *Century's* problems could be solved by a modernized layout. In addition, Frank urged Schuster to institute a new department devoted exclusively to postwar European affairs, which he confidently predicted would hold the attention of Americans for many years to come. In short, Frank envisioned a literary magazine with broad appeal, mass circulation, and correspondingly large profits.[4]

Frank and his ideas won Schuster's enthusiastic support. In April, 1921, Schuster made Frank editor-in-chief at an annual salary of $13,000, telling the readers that "As author, publicist, and lecturer he is known to a large and increasing audience. . . . We commit *The Century* into his hands with confidence and high hopes."[5] The promotion gave Frank virtual control over what appeared in the magazine, and thrust him, at the age of thirty-four, into the front rank of New York editors. "I could not be freer," wrote the elated Frank, "were I editing a private journal for my own reading in the jungles of Africa."[6]

Frank wasted no time in changing the magazine's appearance. He redesigned the cover, which under the previous editor had varied from issue to issue. For the muddy reds and greens, the nondescript artwork, and the Ionic column and American flag borders, Frank substituted a standarized soft-brown cover which contained the name of the magazine, the date and number of issue, and the Century Company's colophon. He retained the old seven-by-nine-inch trim size and the two-column format, but he substituted a larger, more modern type face for the text of the articles. He did not departmentalize the magazine. He left it much as before, with a lead fiction article followed by more fiction, current-event pieces, editorial comment, book reviews, and advertisements. But he employed contemporary black-and-white drawings and charcoal sketches in place of poorly reproduced photographs and color reproductions of old masterpieces. His changes in format at once modernized and dignified the magazine, which had lost some of its original flavor under a succession of editors.

Frank was no less thorough in giving luster to the contents of the magazine. In place of dated articles on "The Little Speckled Hen" and "Our Village" he featured the latest short stories of Sinclair Lewis, the poetry of Stephen Vincent Benét, and the acid political commentary of H. L. Mencken. The writings of John Lowery Simpson and Phyllis Bottome gave way to those of Zona Gale, Sara Teasdale, and Hamlin Garland. The *Century* rapidly became a forum for such diverse political figures as the radical Socialist

Eugene Debs, the middle-of-the-road William McAdoo, and the arch-conservative Edward W. Bok. Frank took particular pleasure in capitalizing on his associations with the chief lecturers of the Chautauqua circuit. Shrewdly sensing the widespread popularity of certain topics and speakers, he solicited contributions from Maurice Hindus on revolutionary Russia, Albert Edward Wiggam on the "New Biology," and Nathaniel Peffer on future events in the Orient.

Eminent though these contributors were, the youthful Frank was not overawed. He did not hesitate to reject manuscripts which he felt did not measure up to the new standards of the *Century*, nor was he reluctant to return those which he felt needed further polishing. On the whole, his authors appreciated the keenness of his editorial eye. Many years later, Maurice Hindus recalled with relief that Frank had turned down an article which emphasized his belief in the stability of the Weimar Republic; and Eugene Debs responded to Frank's critical suggestions with a politeness which bordered on humility.[7]

Frank did, of course, make some errors in judgment. In 1922, for example, he published an article by a former governor of Indiana, James P. Goodrich, who predicted that the Soviet Union under Lenin would soon abandon communism for capitalism and would strive for improved relations with the United States. And, laboring under the pressure of a monthly deadline, Frank also continued to run "filler" fiction by writers of lesser reputation such as Konrad Bercovici, Garet Garrett, and Thomas Beer. On balance, however, the magazine's appearance and contents materially improved under Frank's editorship.

The stamp of Glenn Frank's personality on the *Century* was evidenced not merely in the striking changes he instituted in format and content, but also in "The Tide of Affairs," the monthly column which he wrote in fulfillment of his original agreement with W. Morgan Schuster. Here Frank recorded "the suspended judgment of one American who has been trying to make himself at home in the modern world, trying to orientate himself among the new forces that are making this time what it is." Without the acrimonious sarcasm or burning wit of an H. L. Mencken, he mildly chided institutions and society. "If in order to be a good American," he said, "I had to adjourn my intelligence and pretend that I thought America flawless, I should prefer to go through life a man without a country."[8]

Developing themes he had touched upon earlier in his *Politics of Industry,* Frank contended that the nation had yet to face the challenges posed by the machine age. Pointing to the Senate's rejection of American membership in the League of Nations, he condemned the fallacious reasoning of provincial politicians who befuddled the electorate by preaching an egotistic nationalism which foolishly ignored the dynamics of political and economic forces at work in other parts of the world. He lamented the fact that in spite of a noisy devotion to popular government, the bulk of the voters displayed only a sporadic and short-lived interest in the issues, now and again supporting reform movements in much the same way a bored housewife might embrace a religious cult. Part of the trouble resulted from the existing constitutional structure, which made it hard for the individual American to trace the effect of his vote on the ultimate policy of the government. The declining influence of the clergy compounded the situation. Frank attributed this to the war's damaging effect upon spiritual faith, to poor clerical salaries that discouraged talented men, to a failure of theological thought to keep pace with modern materialism, and to reactionary elements intent on using the Scriptures as a "spiritual cocaine" designed to deaden the aspirations of the masses.[9]

Frank tempered his views with the contention that the United States was on the verge of a "Spiritual Renaissance" based on cultural nationalism, economic internationalism, democratized industry, liberalized business, rationalized politics, and socialized religion. The leaders of this "fine flowering of modern thought" would be enlightened industrial leaders, neither burdened with the exacting details of administration nor entangled in the exigencies of party politics. They would be dedicated to the larger aims of using their businesses consciously to promote the "social virtues" of efficiency, of justice, and of sanity. To help pave the way for the masses' acceptance of these industrial statesmen, he called upon the major political parties to establish nonpartisan committees to formulate platforms dealing with reality; he asked the clergy to lead a religious revival by talking directly to the people; he proposed the establishment of community forums to diffuse knowledge; and he suggested that science find the means to breed all races to a higher level.[10]

Frank was neither an original nor a profound thinker. His reputation was based primarily upon his capacity to state fairly obvious truth in language which seemed to make it more significant than it really was. Quite often, of course, he succeeded in translating relatively complex sociological and economic concepts into terms that were readily understood by both the readers of the *Century* and the audiences on the lecture circuit. To some extent, Frank's inability to probe more deeply the issues of the day reflected his crowded schedule and his lack of time for serious reflection. Then, too, as a practical man, Frank was not one to discard a successful speech, a polished paragraph, or a telling phrase. He repeated them time without number in speeches, in articles, and in his columns, and finally he republished them in a book entitled *An American Looks at His World*.[11] Apart from the fame which these activities brought him (a matter of no small moment to Glenn Frank), he was always conscious of the financial rewards which his speaking engagements and literary efforts could produce.

Between 1920 and 1924 Frank earned, on the average, $25,000 a year. Almost half this amount came from the sale of magazine articles, from book royalties, and from speaking engagements. Lecturing was easily his most lucrative outside source of income. His standard honorarium was

$350, a sum which organizations throughout the country were glad to pay for his services. Colleges and universities—notably his alma mater, Northwestern—sometimes obtained Frank as a commencement speaker with the lure of an honorary degree, an inducement to which he was peculiarly susceptible. But it was the money which most attracted him, and as the demand for his services increased, so too did his willingness to squeeze all that he could from his reputation. Thus he told his agent, Louis Alber, on May 5, 1924: "Let me know the most we can nick them for and we will see whether we can fit the date in."[12] Fully appreciating the market for his talents, he once earned $5,000 in a single week, and in 1925 he signed a contract to write a daily newspaper column for the McClure Syndicate. It promised to push his income over $30,000 a year.

In marked contrast to his experience in Boston, as editor, lecturer, and publicist, Frank now moved easily in New York society. He appeared at many literary parties, where his witty urbanity enabled him to sparkle even in the presence of famous novelists and poets. Too, the Franks made their uptown apartment a fashionable meeting place for influential people from the world of publishing, politics, and business. Among their most frequent visitors were such editors, authors, and critics as Oswald Garrison Villard, Hamilton Holt, Zona Gale, Margaret Ayer Barnes, and Mark and Carl Van Doren, all of whom enjoyed the fireside conversations which invariably followed the sumptuous dinners. In the course of his work with the League to Enforce Peace, Frank had become acquainted with numerous political and business leaders, and now, as editor of the *Century,* he continued to cultivate these relationships. He frequently called on the New York banker, Frank A. Vanderlip, occasionally lunched with John D. Rockefeller, Jr., and once vacationed in Maine with the financier Thomas Lamont. Although at this time Frank showed no active political aspirations, he was in touch with the ranking figures in Democratic circles. William McAdoo, a presidential aspirant in 1924, sought his advice;

Franklin D. Roosevelt, crippled by polio but still a power in the party, discussed Democratic strength with him; and Alfred E. Smith, governor of New York, chatted with him on a first-name basis. Frank's espousal of enlightened capitalism and his continuing interest in the Social Gospel provided the basis for many conversations with Norman Thomas, whom he met frequently and who considered Frank a "true liberal."[13]

To all appearances, Glenn Frank had realized all his ambitions. He took pleasure in editing the *Century*, in expounding his ideas as a freelance journalist, in lecturing to appreciative audiences, and in knowing people who were in the news. He thrived on all that New York had to offer—the skyscrapers, the clamor of rush-hour traffic, the theater openings, and the rococo elegance of fine restaurants. Above all, he savored the status and prestige which the diverse facets of his career commanded.

But satisfying though the rich and varied New York life was, Frank's aspirations were in a continual state of flux. So long as he was in Missouri, a career as a Billy Sunday had seemed an adequate goal. Northwestern enlarged his world, and with it his ambitions. Boston and New York opened successive vistas, and he adjusted his sights accordingly. In 1919 the associate editorship of the *Century* had seemed an important step upwards, and he had demonstrated creative ingenuity in the difficult task of rejuvenating the magazine. But he had failed to reckon with the fact that the day of the literary periodical was over. At best, Frank merely succeeded in slowing the magazine's decline in circulation, and by 1925 he sensed that he had carried his editorial career to its limits, that the *Century* no longer afforded the springboard he had once supposed. The inner compulsion which had driven him to this pinnacle now obliged him to seek other summits to conquer.

V

The University of Wisconsin

IN MARCH, 1925, GLENN FRANK received an informal inquiry about his availability for the presidency of the University of Wisconsin. He read the letter with considerable interest, and though he knew Madison to be only a middle-sized college town and state capital, he found himself intrigued with the proposal. Whatever the drawbacks of relocating in the Midwest, the presidency of the best-known state university in America clearly represented a substantial advance over the editorship of even so renowned a periodical as the *Century*. The University also promised to give Frank an aura of intellectual respectability and authority—something which his successive careers as alumni secretary, speechwriter, lecturer, and editor had failed to provide. For all his wealth and prestige, the former preacher from Green Top felt that the scholarly community somehow considered him a mere publicist and popularizer. And well they might have, for Frank was prone to lumping careers in journalism and higher education together, as if they embodied values of the same order.[1] Now, with his confidence buttressed by a record unblemished by failure, he never for a moment doubted his capacity to undertake so responsible a task as molding the development of a great institution of higher learning.

Nevertheless, he reacted cautiously. In the first place, he had no way of knowing how seriously to treat the tentative, unofficial inquiry. It had come from Zona Gale, one of

46

the *Century's* most illustrious contributors, then a fifty-year-old spinster and resident of Portage, Wisconsin. As the state's most prominent literary figure, Miss Gale had been appointed to the University's governing body, the Board of Regents, in 1923. Her fame rested primarily upon the romanticized picture of small-town life which she depicted in her novels, plays, and short stories. Her most famous novel, *Miss Lulu Bett,* was adapted for the stage and won a Pulitzer prize in 1921. She had become acquainted with Frank in the early twenties, first in an author-editor relationship and then as a close family friend. The gentle, retiring Zona frequently dined at the Franks' apartment and delighted in their companionship. Indeed, she behaved rather like a maiden aunt to Frank, fawning over him and extolling him as a man of tremendous intellectual attainment and administrative ability. Frank, though touched that Zona Gale should think him qualified as a "liberal" and "progressive" spokesman to guide the destinies of the University, realized that she was acting not only without the consent of the Board of Regents, but also without its knowledge.

Conditions in Madison also gave Frank pause. He knew that trouble was brewing behind the tree-shaded facade of the University of Wisconsin, and he felt constrained to weigh the competing advantages and disadvantages of the presidency before seriously exploring the vacancy. The major attraction lay in the University's tradition, particularly in its devotion to academic freedom and its record of service to the people of the state. In 1894 the Board of Regents had issued a ringing declaration of principle: "We cannot . . . believe that knowledge has reached its final goal, or that the present condition of society is perfect. . . . In all lines of academic investigation it is of the utmost importance that the investigators should be absolutely free to follow the indicators of truth wherever they may lead. Whatever may be the limitations which trammel inquiry elsewhere we believe the great State University of Wisconsin should ever encourage that continual and fearless sifting and winnowing by which alone the truth can be found." In 1925 the University had eight thousand students, an annual budget of several million dollars, and a faculty of six hundred. There were many renowned teachers and researchers at the University, including John R. Commons in economics, Charles K. Leith in geology, Edward A. Ross in sociology, and Carl Russell Fish in history.

Ironically, the driving force which had brought the University to the forefront of American educational institutions had been a political one, and in 1925 it was the divisiveness of politics which threatened its integrity. At the turn of the century, Governor Robert M. La Follette launched a program designed to make the University a dynamic instrument of social change. As La Follette saw it, the University constituted a vast reservoir of technical knowledge which the state ought to utilize in the formulation of public policy. In 1903 the governor dictated the choice of a close friend, Charles R. Van Hise, as president. A geologist, Van Hise readily accepted La Follette's principle that the boundaries of the University were the boundaries of the state, and encouraged his faculty to participate actively in furthering "The Wisconsin Idea." The La Follette Progressives had drawn heavily upon University experts in framing and administering legislation to regulate corporate wealth, and this marriage of education and politics had more than anything else given the University of Wisconsin its international reputation as a pioneer in social and economic reform.

But the use of the University as an arm of state government had produced some unexpected consequences. It had plunged the institution into political controversy and had tended to link its fortunes with those of the Progressives. By 1917 the Progressives had lost control of Wisconsin, and their influence within the University had waned accordingly. Nevertheless, La Follette, now a United States Senator, continued to regard the University as his fiefdom, and he was particularly incensed that President Van Hise and the overwhelming majority of the faculty and students vigorously denounced his anti-war policy. "I strongly believe," declared Van Hise, that "the policies of Senator La Follette . . . are dangerous to the country." The senator's two sons, Robert, Jr., and Philip Fox, looked on in cold fury as University students burned an effigy of their father, and they carefully recorded the names of all those faculty members who signed the "round robin" petition censuring his alleged pro-German sympathies.

After the war the University functioned in an atmosphere of conflict and antagonism. The sudden death of Van Hise in November, 1918, further complicated matters, for the presidency passed to a non-Progressive, Edward A. Birge. A member of the faculty since 1876, the sixty-seven-year-old limnologist was rich in administrative experience, having served for many years as dean of the College of Letters and Sciences and as acting president from 1901 to 1903. But Birge was too old and too engrossed in his study of aquatic invertebrates to give the University the direction it needed or to heal the wounds of factionalism. Anyway, he considered himself as merely an interim executive. He appreciated that increasing enrollments and rising costs had created additional problems for the University, but he felt that changes "should be undertaken by a man in middle life, who is in close and sympathetic touch with the men of his own age."

Although Zona Gale did not give him precise details, Glenn Frank knew that the critical problems facing the University would be inherited by Birge's successor. The interim president had failed to act on proposals to reorganize the structure of various schools, had balked at raising faculty salaries in line with postwar prices, had postponed major administrative appointments, and had neglected to press the state legislature for increased appropriations. Birge had also nettled the Progressives by failing to carry forward the Van Hise program for increased University participation in the affairs of the state. Senator La Follette and his allies charged that the University had grown "conservative," a criticism which guided the Progressives following their

return to office in 1920. Their first step was to use their
appointive power to give the Board of Regents of the University a strong Progressive cast by filling vacancies with
adherents of "The Wisconsin Idea." Though the Progressives on the Board readily recognized the need for a younger, more aggressive president, they hesitated until 1924 to
press for Birge's resignation out of deference to his many
years of distinguished service to the institution.

The Board announced that Birge would retire in June,
1925, and appointed a five-member subcommittee to nomi-
nate candidates to succeed him. The complexion of the subcommittee reflected the Progressive orientation of the University's governing body after 1920. Theodore Kronshage,
Jr., president of the Board and chairman of the nominating
committee, was a Milwaukee lawyer, public utilities ex-
pert, and for many years a close friend and confidant of
the elder La Follette. Kronshage had three allies: John
Callahan, the state superintendent of public instruction and
secretary of the committee; Daniel Grady, a Portage lawyer
who had made his reputation as the prosecuting counsel in
a series of Wisconsin anti-trust suits; and Zona Gale. The
only non-Progressive was Henry Butler, a Madison busi-
nessman whose term as Regent expired during the course of
the committee's deliberations. He was replaced by Michael
B. Olbrich, a former chairman of the Wisconsin Republican
party who had twice placed La Follette's name in nomination
for the presidency of the United States.[2]

From the outset, there was speculation that the committee
lacked a will of its own—that it was hand-picked merely to
ratify La Follette's choice. Some faculty members even believed that La Follette coveted the post for himself, so that
he might, among other things, proscribe his wartime critics.
Such fears proved groundless; the senator had no intention
of abandoning his political career at a time when the White
House seemed within his grasp. He contented himself with
expressing his preference for Robert Morss Lovett, the liberal
dean of the University of Chicago. But Lovett declined to

be considered for the presidency, reportedly after John R. Commons had told him that "A Christian like you wouldn't last a week."[3] The dean's refusal was symptomatic of the reluctance of talented academic administrators to risk embroilment in the partisan political controversies associated with the University of Wisconsin.

It took the nominating committee several months to propose a second candidate, Roscoe Pound, the eminent dean of the Harvard Law School. On January 21, 1925, the Board of Regents heartily endorsed his candidacy, and preliminary correspondence indicated that Pound's acceptance was a foregone conclusion. The subcommittee immediately left for Cambridge, formally to offer him the presidency and to make the final arrangements. The dean heard the Madison delegation out, confirmed the Regents' impression of his serious interest, and requested a few days to reflect upon the details. President Birge sent his congratulations to the president-elect, and someone informed the press.[4] Then, to the surprise and embarrassment of the University and its Regents, Pound rejected the offer.

Publicly, the dean announced on February 2 that he wished to devote his life to legal scholarship rather than to academic administration, and that his wife shrank from the duties implicit in the presidency of a large university. Privately, however, in a letter of January 27 to the secretary of the subcommittee, Pound indicated the two considerations which had weighed most heavily with him. First of all, the dean wrote, "It is urged that I cannot honorably withdraw from the Harvard Law School at this time in view of a project for [its] development which was set on foot at my instance, and is represented to be absolutely dependent on my continued connection with the School." Secondly, and no less important, there was the political situation in Madison. "Confidential advice has come to me from Wisconsin," continued Pound, "that I should be regarded as the choice of a party, and should have to expect political difficulties in the near future. When I put this to Miss Gale yesterday, I was much disturbed at her answer. She said that the present Board of Regents would hold for six years to come, and hence tenure was assured. Very likely tenure would be assured, but I could not consent to go to an institution of learning as the choice of a party, or where I should be regarded as such. I had assumed a situation entirely divorced from politics, and the information I now have as to the intimate relation of university and its conduct to politics comes as a distinct shock."[5]

When the dismay at Dean Pound's renunciation of the presidency subsided, the Regents turned almost inevitably to Glenn Frank. Zona Gale, whose unguarded description of the University climate had halted so abruptly the negotiations with Pound, championed Frank's candidacy. He had been her first choice from the outset. As early as June, 1924, she had urged the nominating committee to seek Edward A. Filene's confidential appraisal of Frank's strengths and weaknesses.[6] Frank did not immediately become an acknowledged contender for the presidency, however, because Filene was in Europe and did not respond until the following October. Although Filene then said that he considered Frank "the best man in the country for your purpose—at least the best man I know of," he also doubted that Frank would be willing to give up his position in New York.[7] The juxtaposition of the late arrival of Filene's evaluation and his discouraging estimate of Frank's availability served to focus the committee's attention on Dean Pound and other more likely prospects. In the fall of 1924, therefore, Frank was but a folder in the committee's file of candidates.

But Zona Gale continued to hope that she could revive the Regents' interest in Frank. In January, 1925, when the nominating committee was in Massachusetts to confer with Pound, she arranged for two of her colleagues, Theodore Kronshage and John Callahan, to meet with Filene at the Copley Plaza Hotel. There Filene repeated substantially what he had written about Frank the preceding October, and a few days later, when Pound declined the presidency, Filene's endorsement of Frank took on significance for the committee members. Zona Gale, sensing the Regents' renewed interest in Frank, was now emboldened to write directly—though still unofficially—to the editor of the *Century*.[8]

Glenn Frank pondered her letter fully two weeks before sending off a carefully phrased reply. He emphasized his commitments in New York, but acknowledged that the presidency of the University of Wisconsin was a tantalizing prospect. "It is the needs and the opportunities of the situation that have captured my interest," he wrote. "If it were simply a case of an easy berth in a thoroughly satisfied and smoothly running institution that presented no challenge, I would not for a moment consider turning my back on the very exciting and profitable contracts that are now awaiting my decision. But I feel that there is a chance to make the University of Wisconsin once more the pioneer that shall give leadership to the whole field of state supported education. I feel that we have only scratched the surface of what a great university can mean in the life of a state. And I feel once the plans and policy of the university are right, it is possible to stir a whole state to sustain enthusiasm and support."[9]

Zona Gale replied on April 14, giving full rein to her effusiveness. The *Century,* she said, "seems such a glittering tool that I thought more than once we hadn't enough to offer." She told Frank that the University had fallen behind—in its intellectual vitality no less than in its construction program—but added, "By the same sign, with our eight thousand students and our past, what a future you could give us." Shyly confessing that she had kept his name before the Regents, she explained that because the Birge administration was drawing to a close, the committee would have to meet soon and take definite action. "And fancy you two being in Madison. . . . I hold my breath at the whole idea," Zona gushed. "Please in the meantime do not lose interest in us . . . ."[10]

Frank's response of April 17 reflected the tug-of-war which was taking place in his mind. He hinted that various journalistic enterprises promised him substantial financial benefits, and that the temptation to remain in New York was very strong. And yet, he said, "through all of this, I have suspected that when the tumult and the shouting dies we shall discover that the schoolmaster is king." It was the "teaching ministry" which had really attracted him to journalism in the first place. "Tonight's mood," he concluded, "tells me that if a great university should present itself in the near future, with adequate funds and freedom to move forward on a creative program, I should undoubtedly turn my back on this next alluring step in journalism."[11]

With Frank's privately expressed interest in the presidency assured, Zona Gale moved quickly to bring about his election. She proposed to Kronshage a committee meeting to consider his candidacy. Although caught by surprise, and having no prior knowledge of Zona's correspondence with Frank, Kronshage agreed. On May 9 the committee reviewed the Frank file, including biographical material gathered by Frank's sponsor and letters of recommendation from Edward Filene and Walter Dill Scott, his former professor of business psychology and then president of Northwestern University. "Dr. Frank is eminently qualified," wrote Scott, "to win the confidence of the alumni and citizens of Wisconsin"; and Filene assured the Regents that Frank possessed "a combination of high scholarship and practical business ability that would be difficult to surpass." These recommendations deeply impressed the committee, and after a brief discussion it was agreed to submit Frank's name to the full Board of Regents. As Zona Gale reported to Frank, "It isn't my place to quote what was said—but I wished you might have heard, for all of it was so uniquely in your praise. . . . Nothing is known, but I cannot help a great hope. Nothing could be more thrilling, I think."[12]

On the morning of May 13 the Board met in a special executive session. The proceedings lasted less than an hour, and the outcome was never in doubt. Indeed, Benjamin F. Faast, one of the two non-Progressives on the Board, did not

President Glenn Frank.

Billy Sunday.

Edward A. Filene.

Zona Gale.

The Robert M.
La Follettes,
junior and senior.

The La Follette family—Robert M., Belle Case, and
Philip—at the funeral of the Senator in 1925.

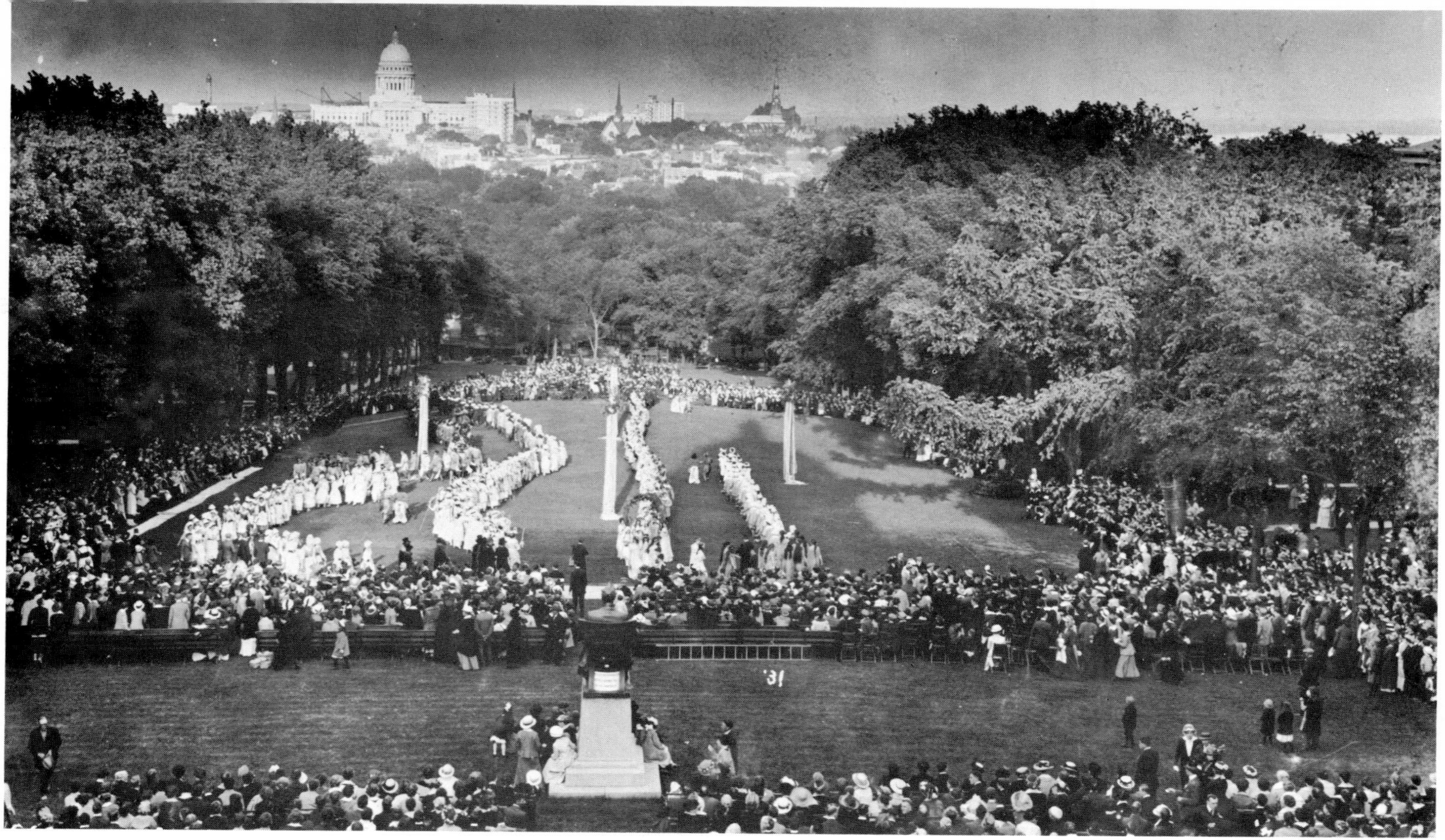

University Archives

Camp Randall Stadium, the site of University football games, about 1920.

*Glenn Frank and Edward A. Birge, photographed at
the time of Frank's arrival in Madison.*

even bother to attend, for he sensed that the La Follette appointees would carry the day. And so it proved. Michael Olbrich, the junior member of the Board, reflected the tone of the meeting by predicting that within two years Glenn Frank would be the most popular figure in the state. "And remember," Olbrich went on, "this man is not merely university presidential timber. He is presidential timber. There is no end to the distance he can go. He has his literary and platform beginning, his ripeness of thought—he is like the figure of the young James Russell Lowell." Next Olbrich, Kronshage, and Callahan read aloud copies of Frank's articles, which the artful Zona Gale had mounted on cardboard for the Regents' convenience. "Listen to this!" they exclaimed in turn, as they competed with each other to quote the most compelling passages from Frank's writings.

Carried away by the enthusiasm of the moment, and doubtless influenced by the sense of urgency implicit in the meeting, the Regents quickly chose Frank for the presidency, instructed the nominating committee to work out the details of a contract, and then adjourned. Strangely, there was no formal election until June 22. As Zona Gale observed, "It was just taken for granted." Even more strange was the fact that the Board made its choice after no more than a brief and cursory examination of Frank's qualifications. The letters from Filene and Scott were the only pieces of disinterested evidence available at the time, and Zona Gale, Frank's most partisan supporter, was the only member of the Board who had ever met him. The Regents seemed convinced that his "progressivism," his personal magnetism, his reputation as a public lecturer, and his record as editor of the *Century* outweighed his obviously limited experience in administering an institution as vast and complex as the University of Wisconsin. Nor did they seem concerned that Frank would be one of the few men to attain the presidency without having served a scholarly apprenticeship within an academic environment.[13]

That day a representative of the Board telephoned Frank

to inform him of the decision. He explained that Kronshage, Olbrich, and Callahan would come to New York to negotiate a contract. This telephone call was Frank's first official contact with the University of Wisconsin—and it gave Zona Gale considerable satisfaction to know that he was not completely unprepared for it.

While Frank waited for the Regents to reach New York, he received two letters containing background information and advice. One came from Zona Gale, who urged him to appoint Theodore Kronshage assistant to the president and warned him that he would probably find the Regents' meetings boring beyond words—concerned, as they were for the most part, with budget matters and appointments.[14] The second letter was from Arnold Hall, a University of Wisconsin professor who had taught Frank economics at Northwestern. "Wisconsin has slumped badly," he reported, because "too many of those in authority . . . have been dominated by what I call the 'divine right of education.' They have not felt that it was their business or duty to sell their product and their ideas to the State of Wisconsin. They have felt that the University owed no particular duty to the people of Wisconsin except in the most abstract and theoretical way."[15] In short, Hall believed that Birge's uninspired administration had vitiated the "Wisconsin Idea," and that Frank, with his well-known flair for the dramatic, was just the man to restore the University's reputation for innovation and public service.

As soon as the Regents arrived in New York they called on Glenn Frank to settle the terms of the presidency. On Frank's desk in the offices of the *Century* lay a conspicuous stack of contracts, and this, combined with the Regents' painful memories of the Pound fiasco, enabled Frank to negotiate from a position of great strength. He asked for and received a salary of $18,000 annually, a figure far in excess of what Birge was receiving and a good deal more than the University had offered Dean Pound. It made Frank one of the highest paid university administrators in the United

States. He also proposed that the University pay him a monthly expense account of $200 (later incorporated into his salary) ; reimburse him for all living expenditures "above the normal family expenses of the president"; provide him with a large, redecorated presidential mansion; defray his moving expenses; and furnish him with a chauffeured automobile. Further, the Regents permitted Frank to fulfill his outstanding lecture engagements—always an important source of additional income. Frank agreed to assume the presidency on September 1, 1925, and offered as soon as possible to withdraw from his commitment to write a daily syndicated newspaper column.[16] With the terms of his appointment settled to his satisfaction, Glenn Frank announced from New York City on May 20 that he had accepted the presidency of the University of Wisconsin.[17]

Immediately, letters and telegrams began to pour in to Frank from all over the country. Politicians, writers, businessmen, and society figures joined in congratulating him and extending him best wishes in his new career. Among his New York circle of acquaintances, the reaction of novelist Fannie Hurst was typical: "The University of Wisconsin has surpassed even its forward looking self. More power to you." Edward A. Ross, the University's distinguished sociologist, described Frank as a discriminating thinker, a well-rounded progressive who had little use for the "slap-dash oversimplified thinking of radicals," and a "reasonable, impersonal and just man of great charm." Editorial reaction in the state was no less enthusiastic. The Madison *Wisconsin State Journal* described him as a scholar and a leader, and the Madison *Capital Times,* the most influential Progressive paper in Wisconsin, predicted that Frank's appointment signaled the advent of a new era for the University.[18] The *Milwaukee Journal* said, "His statements show an earnest desire to conserve and develop the University. His training and equipment would point to his becoming an interpreter of the school to the state and the state to the university."

The enthusiasm, though widespread, was not universal.

President Birge's letter promising his co-operation and extending his best wishes was brief to the point of curtness. George Clarke Sellery, the influential dean of the College of Letters and Sciences, expressed private reservations: that he and other "older" faculty members had hoped for someone from within the academic community for their president. And rumor had it that Frank's appointment did not entirely reflect Senator La Follette's wishes.[19] The measure of Frank's ability would be his capacity over the next few months and years to dispel the misgivings which these reactions implied.

On Sunday morning, June 25, Glenn Frank arrived in Madison on a brief exploratory visit. As he stepped down from the railway coach at the North Western station, he looked subtly but unmistakably larger than life—almost a caricature of an urbane, successful Easterner. At thirty-seven he was young for a university president, and in some respects his face accentuated his youth: unlined, somewhat soft and plastic, as if his dominant features were still in the process of forming. But his receding hairline, which was made the more noticeable by the height and prominence of his forehead, seemed to suggest that he was older than his years, and his obvious effort to conceal his growing baldness only strengthened this impression. Above all, it was his eyes which gave a presidential cast to his expression. Dark and deeply set, they seemed alight with vital magnetism. His clothes also set him apart, and as he stepped into the heat of Madison his faintly dandified attire struck an incongruous note. Even by New York standards, Frank tended ever so slightly to overdress, and in this small midwestern city he instantly established a reputation for sartorial elegance. He was wearing a gray fedora, a fashionably cut blue suit, a fawn-colored chinchilla overcoat, black patent-leather shoes, and—despite the heat—a pair of pearl-gray spats.

Regents Kronshage and Olbrich stepped forward to greet him, and Frank left the station surrounded by a throng of newsmen and curious spectators. A tiring round of conferences, luncheons, and sightseeing filled the next two days. Frank learned nothing new about conditions at the University during his stay, but he was able to take back to his wife in New York a detailed impression of what their life as the presidential family would be like in Wisconsin's capital city.[20]

The campus sprawled across a thousand acres of land bordering on the shores of Lake Mendota, largest of the four lakes which surrounded Madison. Frank's tour took him to every corner of the University. It began with the main administrative and classroom building, Bascom Hall, a large, white-columned structure which stood on a bluff above the lake and faced east toward the Capitol, a mile distant. To the rear, narrow roads wound past the new University Hospital, the Extension Building, the School of Agriculture, and the tile-roofed dormitories. To the north, dense woods screened the lakeshore. To the south, Bascom hill dropped away to classroom buildings, dormitories, University Avenue, the School of Engineering, and Camp Randall Stadium, where the Wisconsin football team had suffered a succession of mediocre seasons. To the front of Bascom Hall, a statue of a pensive Abraham Lincoln gazed eastward over a steeply sloping grass mall which was lined by a conglomeration of architectural forms: the eighty-year-old North and South halls with their clean, straight lines; the rambling structure which housed the department of education; the garish, single-turreted Law School; the Victorian-style Music Hall; and Science Hall, a great red beast of a building which squatted at the foot of the hill. Below the mall on the lower campus was a dormitory, the University Club, an antiquated gymnasium, the State Historical Society of Wisconsin (which also housed the University library), and Langdon Street, with its faculty homes and fraternity and sorority houses. Frank nodded approvingly over all that he saw, expressing particular satisfaction with the University Hospital.

In 1925 Madison had a population of forty thousand people. Most of them lived in the plain, two- and three-story flats which stood in monotonous rows along the tree-lined streets, or in the small, one-family houses which speculative builders had constructed in the residential districts recently platted by real estate promoters. A few, however, lived in the ten- and twenty-thousand-dollar mansions which graced the outlying suburbs, especially along the lake fronts. Still, Madison was far from being a typical "Main Street" or "Middletown." For one thing, the lakes and the wooded hills gave the city an uncommon beauty. More importantly, the legislature, the state offices, and the University combined to give Madison an importance, a vitality, and an intellectual flavor which other Wisconsin communities—even Milwaukee—lacked. To be sure, the "Four Lakes City" was not Boston or New York, but if Frank had any misgivings about leaving the East he certainly showed no signs.

The president-elect summed up his feelings in a statement issued on the eve of his departure for New York. He praised Madison, lauded Birge's contributions to higher education, extolled the University's heritage, and promised to carry forward the Wisconsin tradition. "If I were selecting a delightful place in which to live," he said, "I could not imagine a more attractive home than Madison. . . . I would be keeping back the truth if I did not say that I am deeply moved by the thought of shouldering . . . the responsibility that has so ably been carried by such a succession of great university presidents culminating in the administration of the distinguished and devoted public servant, President Birge. [The] worthy traditions of the University of Wisconsin are a priceless heritage, not only to Wisconsin but to the whole nation. And to have the opportunity to share in its protection and in its promotion is an honor and a genuine call to duty that no man who seriously wants to give his best to his day and generation could do other than answer."[21]

Glenn Frank left Madison keenly aware of the difficulties that lay ahead. He knew that many people considered him a political appointee, hired by the Progressives to transform the University to their liking; he knew that others thought him too young, or too inexperienced, or too unscholarly to be a university president; and he knew that still others, if not actively opposed to his appointment, would be watching him carefully over the coming months. But it was in Frank's nature to make light of such difficulties. After all, his record in Evanston, Boston, and New York had made him supremely confident that he possessed the formula for success.

VI

President Glenn Frank

IT WAS SEPTEMBER 1, 1925: circus day in Madison. The Ringling Bros., Barnum & Bailey Circus trooped around the Capitol Square, where thousands of people gathered to watch a long parade of blaring bands, snarling lions, prancing horses, whistling calliopes, plodding elephants, and cavorting clowns. Amid this general commotion, few people noticed another arrival a few blocks away at the North Western Railroad station. There, within earshot of the strains of circus music, Glenn Frank arrived to assume the presidency of the University of Wisconsin. Impeccable as always, Frank wore a blue striped suit, somewhat English in cut, and a blue figured shirt with a matching tie. These were boldly accented by a grey homburg with a wide black band and highly polished black shoes. Because of the unseasonably hot weather he did not wear his usual spats. At his side were his wife and eight-year-old son, a uniformed maid, and a spotted mongrel dog named Jonsey.

No formal ceremony of welcome marked the occasion, but Zona Gale, who had come forty miles from Portage, added a spontaneous touch of informality by greeting Mrs. Frank with a hug and a kiss, and a cluster of reporters crowded around the new president in the hope of securing some impromptu remarks for the evening editions. Frank had prepared for just such an eventuality. With the efficiency expected of a successful New York editor, he distributed a

70

mimeographed statement which read: "I am here and eager to go to work. . . . We must see to it that this University ever safeguards the right of its scholars to conduct their investigations without fear of consequences." This done, Frank and his party, carefully avoiding Capitol Square, motored to the fashionable Loraine Hotel, which would be their home for two weeks, until painters and interior decorators finished renovating the presidential mansion.[1]

Though momentarily overshadowed by the excitement of circus day, Frank's arrival evoked considerable interest, both in Madison and throughout the state. People hardly knew what to expect of their thirty-seven-year-old "boy president," selected by the Regents from outside the academic community. How well would he fit into provincial Madison? Could he direct the University's fortunes in a difficult transitional period? How would he administer the University? What changes did he contemplate? Could his occasional writings on higher education be taken as a preview of the policies he would follow? What had he meant when he had denounced politically controlled "reptile universities," "sterile Ph.D. training," and "illiberal curriculums"? He had once said that "A really great governor or a really great university president can go far toward driving the knowledge of the university and the power of the state abreast."[2] Did he mean that he approved of the "Wisconsin Idea"? These and many other questions demanded answers.

Both daily newspapers in Madison speculated on these questions. The publisher of the sometimes progressive *Wisconsin State Journal* contended that Frank's writings and speeches demonstrated his courage to take a stand on controversial issues. "If we have acquired a proper sense of President Frank," he wrote, "we are safe in saying that the essential thing in his career has been his pursuit of the truth." Describing the variety of ideas found in Frank's writings, the publisher explained, "In one article the reactionaries may have found discontent and the radicals delight. Perhaps in the next issue there came a complete reversal with the conservatives pleased and the progressives displeased." William T. Evjue, editor of the *Capital Times,* viewed Frank differently. "He has not brought, in a suitcase, a program FOR Wisconsin into which he plans to shove and steer the institution, according to the plans and specifications of his own particular blueprint. . . . In other words, Dr. Frank will be the guiding spirit in a program that will not be made FOR Wisconsin in advance, but which will come out of Wisconsin in her efforts to attain the ideas of this great institution."[3] Evjue's statement was extremely important, for his newspaper frequently reflected the views of the La Follette family. With good reason people called him the "Chief Thunderer of the Progressive faction." His opinions suggested what the Progressive leaders expected of the new president.

Frank's behavior during his first month in Madison did not put an end to the speculation about his policies, but he gave every indication of becoming an active president, one who would make full use of his easy friendliness, urbane manner, and facility with words to secure support for his program whatever it might be. He began by cultivating the friendship of the influential and by making numerous speeches and public appearances. He even led the University band at a football game, to the delight of thousands of onlookers. In his speeches, he carefully avoided controversy. In one, delivered at the Madison Rotary Club on the subject of "One Hundred Per Cent Americanism," he told his audience of businessmen that "Americanism can not be graded by percentages, but has an undefinable, 'spiritual essence.'" In another, made at the official opening of the University's fall term, he warned his twelve hundred "fellow freshman" that their "new world of allurement and challenge" was not "built around a ballroom," but rather existed to make them "creative competitors in the making of the world as it ought to be." Only once did he hint at his approach to the University's problems. He told a newspaper reporter, "I haven't any philosophy, philosophies are generalizations. Just as has been found by teachers of law, I find the best results in approaching the problems of life, both personal and public, can not be obtained by adopting the 'case system.' This is a fluid world. There are a few fixed things like the multiplication tables, but taking life by and large, a conclusion sound today may be unsound next week because the facts or our knowledge of the facts may change in the meantime."[4]

Frank was as aware as his interviewer that a host of complex problems faced him in his new administration: problems created by an alert and skeptical student body; problems of recruiting and keeping an able faculty; of securing and maintaining the support of the governor and legislature; of coping with the varied pressures on the University from business, labor, agriculture, and other interest groups; and uppermost, of maintaining an effective working relationship with the leaders of the Wisconsin Progressive movement. Privately, Frank mused on the various roles these problems would make him play. "The post requires a man to be a sort of synthetic product made up of a travelling salesman, a circus barker, a real estate promoter, a wooden doll at county fairs at which everyone feels impelled to throw something, a politician, a diplomat, and, in spare moments, an educator who takes a sort of platonic interest in things of the mind and spirit."[5] To meet the challenges of this "hazardous occupation," Frank planned to explore the "atmosphere" of the University, to study the "stage setting," and to establish contact with all social classes so that he would be more than a theorist cloistered from the daily swirl of thought and action.[6]

Although in the largest sense Frank was ultimately responsible, through their elected representatives, to the people of Wisconsin, his immediate superiors were the fifteen members of the Board of Regents. Under state law they directed the affairs of the University. Appointed by the governor with the consent of the legislature, they served staggered six-year terms. By law they came from various parts of the state, and traditionally they represented a cross section of Wisconsin life. The Board usually contained a number of people of outstanding ability and intellect. In 1925 it included educators, representatives of various ethnic groups, farmers, a novelist, a Protestant minister, a lawyer, a land speculator, and several manufacturers. Some Regents considered their positions to be merely honorary, but others took their obligations very seriously. Since historically the Board had been subject to public pressure in formulating policy, and since more than one president had been removed from office for political reasons, Frank realized from the start that he could never expect to enjoy the security of tenure and that his actions would always be subject to partisan political scrutiny.

More than any of their recent predecessors, the Regents who hired Frank mirrored the Progressive viewpoint. This meant that he would not only have to perform the normal duties expected of a president—create a favorable public impression, formulate a biennial budget, supervise personnel, handle day-to-day matters, deal with the faculty, and evolve educational policy—but would also have to follow a policy designed to please the Progressives, while at the same time keeping the University from direct involvement in partisan politics. Several of the Board's leading members, notably Theodore Kronshage and Michael Olbrich, played active political roles in Wisconsin, and they co-operated closely with Progressives in the constitutional offices and in the legislature. Moreover, because of a combination of old friendships and loyalties, they listened carefully to any proposals made concerning the University by members of the La Follette family. Although Robert M. La Follette had died in June, 1925, his widow followed the affairs of the University closely, as did the two La Follette boys, Robert M. La Follette, Jr., who fell heir to his father's seat in the United States Senate, and Philip Fox La Follette, who was later to join the University law faculty. Even had he wanted to, therefore, Frank could not have escaped from the seemingly brooding presence of La Follette on the campus.

Various other state organizations took an active interest in the University, and they posed other problems to an incoming president. The Wisconsin Farm Bureau Federation and the Wisconsin Dairy Association, for example, worked closely with the College of Agriculture and its Agricultural Extension Division. The leaders of the two farm organizations had distinct views on how the University should serve the agricultural community and they exercised considerable influence in the legislature. Other interest groups—the State Medical Society, the Wisconsin Taxpayer's Alliance, the various state and local chambers of commerce, and certain large Wisconsin industries—all had their own ideas about how and for whose benefit the University should be operated. Besides the organizations of this type, there was also an official body, the Board of Visitors. Its members had no other function than that of visitation and recommendation; they reported annually to the Board of Regents on the quality of instruction at the University. In general, these observations seemed to vary little from year to year and few people in authority took the recommendations seriously. The private interest groups could not be treated so lightly, however, and Frank quickly found that it required all of his not inconsiderable diplomatic skill to prevent the University from becoming dominated by one or more of the various pressure groups which made demands upon it.

For administrative purposes, the University was divided into a number of semi-autonomous professional schools, divisions, and colleges, administered by deans or directors. In 1925 the deans were Frederick E. Turneaure in the College of Engineering, Harry D. Russell in the College of Agriculture, Harry S. Richards in the Law School, Charles Bardeen in the Medical School, Charles S. Slichter in the Graduate School, Louis Reber in the Extension Division, and George Sellery in the College of Letters and Science. All of these men were administrators of long experience. Turneaure, an authority on bridge construction and structural engineering, had headed the College of Engineering since 1902. Richards, a lawyer from Iowa, had come to the Law School in 1903 and had been dean since then. Russell, a bacteriologist, and Bardeen, a professor of anatomy, had received their appointments in 1907, while Reber, who was largely responsible for building up the Extension Division, had received his deanship in 1910. Slichter, a professor of mathematics, had only become dean of the Graduate School in 1920, but he had been a faculty member since 1889. Sellery, a professor of history, had joined the faculty in 1904 and had assumed direction of the College of Letters and Science in 1919.

Most of these deans and the units of the University which they directed presented no special problems to the incoming president. The deans were so accustomed to carrying out their duties and the general lines of the University's direction of development seemed so well settled that it seemingly made little difference to them who occupied the presidency. Of course, there were rivalries between deans over program priorities and budgets, but the general atmosphere of the University was one of harmony and good will, and there seemed to be no good reason why a skillful president would not be able to reconcile conflicting interests. Indeed, provided their respective schools and colleges received adequate allocations of funds, most deans were perfectly content with existing arrangements, and a few had been in office so long that they preferred to be left alone until they reached retirement.

There was one important exception. George Sellery, a formidable, domineering, but extremely able historian and administrator, more than any of the other deans considered himself a representative of the faculty within the administration. Over the preceding six years, from 1919 to 1925, he had had the ear of President Birge, and he had become used to exerting considerable influence over the formulation of policy. Throughout, he had steadfastly opposed abrupt changes in direction, and he had been deeply angered by the Progressive criticism of Birge's administration. From the very first, he suspected that Frank had been brought in to do the bidding of Progressive politicians. He resented that Frank came from outside the faculty, deplored Frank's non-academic background, and, some believed, felt slighted at having been passed over in favor of Frank for the presidency. If he chose to do so, as Dean of the College of Letters and Science, Sellery was in a position to obstruct Frank's administration.

Although he was keenly aware that the success of his presidency depended very much upon the speedy establishment of a good working relationship with Dean Sellery, from the beginning Frank alienated Sellery without really understanding why. A major cause was a gross tactical error which Frank made before he even came to Madison. Anxious to learn all he could about conditions in the state, in the city, and in the University, he hired a private detective agency to compile dossiers on leading politicians, businessmen, and faculty members. In the early weeks of his administration, Frank compounded this indiscretion by proudly showing the completed file, some forty pages of reports, to Sellery. The dean noted, "The reports were not always complimentary; mine wasn't. Mr. Frank read out a dozen or so and then let me leaf the pages. I got the impression that he was confident that he had a satisfactory grasp on the dominant currents of opinion in the State."[7] Sellery considered Frank's actions a shocking breach of ethics and believed that they provided additional evidence of the president's fundamental lack of understanding of the nature of academic life. This rift between Frank and Sellery never healed. Throughout the next ten years, their relationship remained cold, stiff, and formal.

The deans of men and women, Scott Goodnight and F. Louise Nardin, presented President Frank with an entirely different set of problems. Many faculty members believed that neither dean possessed the personality and outlook appropriate to the supervision of student affairs. Miss Nardin was viewed by some as an unstable woman with such dogmatic, mid-Victorian views on sex that she admonished co-eds not to bend over at drinking fountains and not to wear red dresses. According to some of his colleagues, Goodnight, who also served as the Director of the Summer Session, had little scholarly ability, a streak of bullheadedness, and sufficient talent only to carry out someone else's orders. All agreed, however, that the task of supervising student activities was an extremely vexatious one and that it was unlikely that any dean would be able to carry out the responsibilities without attracting criticism from some section of the University or the general public.

The central problem facing deans Nardin and Goodnight, of course, was the one which most American institutions of higher education still face—in guiding the development of students, what is the proper balance between freedom and restraint? Although the University of Wisconsin had a well-rounded program of cultural and athletic activities, the deans of men and women did not consider it their chief function to co-ordinate and encourage such programs. Rather they saw themselves in a much more negative light, as campus policemen with the responsibility for maintaining discipline and for apprehending and punishing offenders. In short, deans Nardin and Goodnight believed themselves to be the guardians of the University's reputation. Upon their shoulders rested the task of convincing the mothers and fathers of Wisconsin that the students lived moral lives while in Madison.

They sought to accomplish this objective by handling serious breaches of discipline—especially cases of sexual misconduct and excessive drinking—with quiet discretion, so that the newspapers would not sensationalize the facts nor depict isolated incidents as typical occurrences. With few exceptions, the students behaved well enough, and over the years the University had achieved a good reputation. To be sure, it never succeeded in allaying the persistent (if vague) rumors of student debauchery, but such has been the fate of every university community since medieval times, and the University of Wisconsin was no exception. On the other hand, the University of Wisconsin was influenced by the steady liberalization of Victorian codes of conduct that had become increasingly evident since the First World War, and President Frank inherited from his predecessor a pair of deans who seemed ill equipped to handle the changing situation. No major scandal had marred the University's reputation since the war, but more than one observer of the Madison scene believed that there would soon be trouble unless the new president overhauled the disciplinary structure.

Frank's freedom of action to deal with this or any other problem was circumscribed by the fact that the Wisconsin faculty played a more important role in institutional affairs than did the faculty of most other major American universities. Over the years teachers and researchers had fought a continuing battle with administrators, regents, and politicians for control of the University. They had won academic freedom, the right to elect departmental chairmen, and a considerable voice in the operation of the institution. At regularly scheduled faculty and departmental meetings, and through such bodies as the important University Committee, the faculty shaped general educational policy, set scholastic standards, and, in general, determined what kind of an institution the University of Wisconsin was to be. Very rarely did the administration go against faculty advice or advance new policies without its support. All members of the staff of instruction with the rank of assistant professor or above constituted the governing faculty. With the exception of certain types of executive session, teachers of lesser rank had a voice but no vote at faculty meetings. Superficially, at least, it appeared that most business was cut and dried and that it was steered through the faculty and committee meetings by a few dominant personalities. Actually, most decisions were made only after the basic principles had been hammered out in a series of informal meetings at luncheons, dinner parties, or over coffee. Individually and collectively, the faculty was always aware of the struggle which had been required to achieve such a strong voice in University affairs. Thus it viewed with suspicion bordering on distrust a new president brought in from the outside, one who lacked both academic credentials and background, and, above all, one who had urged changes in American higher education. Frank, it seemed, intended to formulate policy in co-operation with the elected representatives of the people rather than with the members of the faculty.

Frank was well aware of the dangers of antagonizing the faculty by acting precipitously, especially in introducing new policies. As adroitly as possible, therefore, he sought to avoid commitments, to disassociate himself from the actions of the Birge administration, to allow the University's internal machinery to "more or less go by momentum," and to convince the faculty that he had absolutely no intention of dictating policy. In keeping with these ideas, he had written to Birge from New York to say that he had no wish to comment upon the budget or any other arrangements proposed for the academic year 1925–1926. He implied that he wished to wait until he had a better idea of the facts and spirit of the situation in the academic community before presuming to contribute to such discussions. Frank also refused to be installed in office formally on the somewhat lame grounds that "an inauguration . . . gives a new president an opportunity to deliver an address that five years later he will wish he had not delivered." When he made his first appearance before the faculty, on October 5, 1925, he again professed his hesitancy about commenting on policy because he believed that all basic decisions affecting the University should result from a collaboration among the president, members of the faculty, the alumni, and, "in a very real sense," the people's representatives. Frank clarified his position somewhat the following month when he told a Madison service club, "It is not my purpose to create a program for the university, but to help Wisconsin fulfill its own program."[8] The new president seemed to be saying that he would be content to administer an institution which had already established its general lines of policy and development. He implied that he would not be an innovator.

But Frank's hope that he would be permitted an extended period in which to familiarize himself with the University before being called upon to formulate policy was quickly shattered. Soon after he reached Madison there arose an acrimonious dispute which forced his hand. At issue was the question of the propriety of the University's accepting gifts from private corporations—in this instance the Rockefeller Foundation's offer in the summer of 1925 to finance new buildings for medical research. The Progressives on the Board of Regents had disagreed among themselves over whether or not to accept the grant. Some had based their opposition on an article which the elder La Follette had written a few months before his death. In what was almost a political last will and testament, he had warned his followers that the Rockefeller Foundation was part of a sinister conspiracy designed to place higher education under the thumb of great wealth. "Our universities, colleges and other educational institutions are cringing and fawning for favors of predatory wealth," wrote the senator. "Big business must be cajoled and propitiated. Money however dirty or rotten is made a God. It may reek with the filth of the sweat-shop, it may represent the labor of little children warped and dwarfed in body and mind. It may be coined from the anguish of broken homes, the horror of the trenches or the hell of war—it cannot be too vile or debased in its source to devote to the cause of higher education." The Progressive Regents who had favored the grant had naturally wanted the University of Wisconsin to stay clear of any alliance with the "Monopoly System," but they had argued that corporate gifts already constituted four per cent of the institution's income, that it was unrealistic to assume that legislative appropriations alone would ever provide enough money for research programs, and that acceptance of corporate money— even that made by coupon-clipping capitalists—did not necessarily entail control of the University by the forces of privilege. Regent Michael Olbrich, a sympathizer with most of La Follette's ideas, had asserted, "We are not a morals squad. Let's be consistent and keep our halo straight if we are going to wear one." In mid-August the Regents had held a stormy four-hour meeting at which the wishes of their dead chief prevailed. They rejected the Rockefeller money by a vote of nine to five and passed a resolution designed to clarify policy on the acceptance of gifts. It stated that "no gifts, donations or subsidies shall in the future be accepted by or on behalf of the University of Wisconsin from any incorporated educational endowments or organizations of like character."[9]

The Board had acted without consulting Frank, who was then busy concluding his affairs in New York. What information he received came unofficially from Olbrich and Zona Gale. Zona, who eventually voted in favor of the resolution, had told Frank in July, "President Birge said that if he were incoming president and such action taken, he should resign." Olbrich had written after the vote, probably to reassure Frank: "The resolution . . . has no binding force or effect in law upon this or any other Board of Regents. The next meeting of the board, if a majority then present willed, is quite as free to receive gifts as they ever were."[10]

When Frank reached Madison at the beginning of September, the Board's decision to reject the Rockefeller Foundation's offer was being hotly debated throughout the Midwest. Columnists in the *Capital Times* and *La Follette's Magazine* hailed the rejection of the "tainted money," but rumors were afloat that some professors intended to resign from the University. An alumni committee started an investigation, many groups passed memorials criticizing the Board's action, and various Regents wrote articles justifying their positions. A distinguished faculty member charged that the refusal to accept research funds threatened to turn the University into a "glorified high school."[11] The controversy threatened to embroil Frank and to force him to choose one side or the other.

To meet the challenge, Frank issued two statements. On one hand he said that he opposed political domination of the University; on the other he cited the need for continuing research. In October, 1925, he informed the faculty, "We must assure to the research of this institution as nearly complete freedom as is humanly possible in an organized society and, as I see it, freedom of research in this institution implies freedom from the influences and the dictates of organized politics." A month later, in a welcoming address before the National Academy of Sciences, he said, "Speaking for the plans and purposes of the administration and for the scientific staff, I can assure you that the University of Wisconsin will neither cut itself off from the vast co-operative efforts of American and European scholarship nor entrench its own research program."[12] Frank's words, while contradictory, were sufficiently vague to satisfy both sides in the dispute. All concerned concluded that Frank agreed with their basic position.

Before Frank had to commit himself further, the Regents compromised. During 1926 they ignored the letter of the resolution and established a policy of accepting gifts from selected sources which in the eyes of the Regents did not deal in "tainted money." These included the Wisconsin Manufacturers' Association, the Quaker Oats Company, and several corporations directed by Progressives. The Regents, moreover, sanctioned the establishment by the alumni of the Wisconsin Alumni Research Foundation (WARF), which solicited research funds from corporate sources. From a practical standpoint, only Rockefeller money seemed taboo. The resolution, which continued for some time to be a controversial item in Wisconsin politics, remained in effect until 1930, when Depression conditions forced the Regents to adopt a more flexible policy. In the meantime, the Board professed to find nothing contradictory in its actions, and

Frank delivered several speeches favoring research programs financed by outside money but unencumbered by controlling restrictions.[13]

Despite Frank's initial caution and his obvious reluctance publicly to commit himself on policy matters, he had really grandiose plans for the University of Wisconsin. In fact, he was so eager to get started along these lines that he soon violated his own operating principles—to play everything very quietly until he was well established and fully understood the local situation. He intended to revolutionize the curriculum of the College of Letters and Science and thereby to revolutionize higher education in America. "Every day I am becoming more convinced that the liberal arts course in our universities is educationally obsolete, and that no tinkering with courses will correct the situation," he wrote in confidence five months after the beginning of his administration. "Unless I am totally at sea in my analysis, I think it will be possible to do here a thing that will have as far reaching an effect upon the liberal education of the next fifty years as the Eliot development of the elective system had on the liberal education of the last fifty years."[14] Clearly, Glenn Frank saw himself as a major educational innovator.

He envisioned the establishment of an experimental college within the University. There he hoped to isolate and experiment with a group of typical freshmen. Those in charge of the project would be under no obligation to respect existing academic traditions, either in curriculum or in method. They would be free to develop "new experimental proof" that would eventually become a standard part of the University's curriculum.[15]

Frank got the idea for the new type of college from Alexander Meiklejohn, a controversial figure in American higher education. A student of classical Greek philosophy, in 1924 Meiklejohn had been dismissed from the presidency of Amherst College following a long battle with its trustees. He had tried to convince the trustees that the faculty should have more control over the expenditure of funds. At the same time he had criticized the faculty for placing their departments ahead of the general welfare of the college. Following his ouster he had lectured and written about educational reform. In January, 1925, his blueprint for an experimental college had appeared in a *Century* article entitled "A New College: Notes on Next Steps in Higher Education." Frank was much taken with the article; he and Meiklejohn had actually discussed the possibility of establishing such a college, but though both men were intrigued by the idea it was not until Frank became president of the University of Wisconsin that it became possible for them to advance their plans. In his first major appointment, Frank named Meiklejohn to a post as Brittingham Professor of Philosophy. The professorship carried a salary of $10,000 a year and was extremely well paid by the standards of the day. "We can make this the most thrilling adventure in America," Frank wrote Meiklejohn.[16]

On March 1, 1926, Frank formally announced to the faculty his plans for the establishment of an experimental college. In language which must have shocked purists among the faculty, he asserted that "the next great advance of education outside the legitimate areas of intensive specializations will be marked by a fluidizing of its present special rigid formalizations, by an extensive informalizing of the teaching process." Whether or not they fully understood Frank's scheme, the faculty quickly referred the proposal to a specially appointed all-University commission, which included Frank and Meiklejohn among its members. The commission gave its approval with almost indecent speed, and in less than two months, on May 22, 1926, the faculty formally voted to establish an experimental college.

But, as Frank was soon to learn, faculty ratification did not necessarily mean that his scheme had been accepted enthusiastically. Few faculty members shared his belief that there was a need for an experimental college; the overwhelming majority agreed to the proposal simply out of good will to the new president: they were willing to let him have his way in a matter which was obviously close to his heart.

But Frank misunderstood the meaning of this endorsement and mistakenly believed that the majority of the faculty shared his enthusiasm. He went ahead with plans for the new college, appointed Meiklejohn director, and delivered a series of speeches attacking traditional methods of educational instruction. While he generally avoided any mention of the University of Wisconsin, many faculty members resented his implied criticism. One day he asked Sellery, "How am I doing?" The dean answered, "You are doing very well, but when you are lecturing on universities I wish you would say 'we' instead of 'they.' That will remind you that the old days of free swinging at the universities are over for you."[18] Frank should have perceived what Sellery was urging, but he neither understood the dean's remark nor recognized its sarcastic overtones.

In June, 1926, Frank completed his first academic year as president of the University of Wisconsin. From several standpoints he considered it successful. He had made public contacts, avoided taking sides in the fund-raising controversy, acquired firsthand knowledge about the operations of the University, and instituted a program of education reform. On the day before graduation a large crowd turned out to hear him deliver a baccalaureate address. Frank's audience expected something special, and it was not disappointed, for it heard an eloquently worded and faultlessly delivered statement of principle. "I covet for the University of Wisconsin great buildings, broad acres, and ample budgets, but only to give worthy shelter and adequate tools to her spirit of eager and unhampered integrity. I would rather see the University of Wisconsin naked and poor, if she but kept her freedom, than to see her clothed and rich if she bought equipment at the price of liberty. And I give the people of Wisconsin this pledge: So long as I remain the president of the

University of Wisconsin, this institution will not, with my consent, either angle for or accept one scintilla of support either from private or from public sources, that implies either an obvious or a legitimately suspected infringement upon the right of the scholars of Wisconsin to pursue their investigations without fear and to publish their findings without fear of consequence."[19] And so Frank closed on a ringing note. But the basic questions had been only partially answered.

VII

In Office

BETWEEN 1926 AND 1929, Glenn Frank impressed the people of Wisconsin as an able, complex, and many-faceted personality. As a university president he directed the development of one of the largest American institutions of higher learning, shrewdly curried the favor of members of the state legislature, promoted educational change, and spoke out in defense of academic freedom. As a public figure he wrote a syndicated newspaper column on national issues and problems, lectured to audiences across the nation, met such famous people as King George V of England and George Bernard Shaw, and reflected on the philosophical implications of the industrial revolution. He also entertained at the presidential mansion, watched his son grow to young manhood, played golf whenever time and weather permitted, and cheered the University of Wisconsin football team from a private box in the stadium. In all of these roles he remained Glenn Frank the publicist, never forgetting to show himself, as well as his ideas, in the best possible light.

Words of praise followed him everywhere. His speeches prompted people to commend his "sound thought," his "unusual facility in the use of language," his "happy faculty of interjecting humor," his mastery of "lexicology," and his ability to hold an audience enthralled. "Indeed," said an observer, "so pleasing does Dr. Frank talk that one is in danger of being blinded by the beauty of his diction, to the

88

truth it undertakes to convey." He received national attention. H. L. Mencken seriously considered him to be a potential candidate for the United States presidency, and other critics applauded his syndicated columns. The La Follette brothers commended his vision and vigor to groups of students and instructors; newspaper editors extolled his worth; one writer even believed that he was better known than the Illinois football star, Red Grange.[1] Frank obviously enjoyed his new life. He did not seem to miss New York City. He liked his job, enjoyed his large home, took pleasure in his ample income, and basked in the roar of the crowd.

There were, of course, a few people who privately expressed dissatisfaction with the way that Frank was running the University, and both his actions and his attitudes occasionally attracted public criticism. Although Frank disregarded most critics, they were straws in the wind, the meaning of which a more perceptive man would readily have appreciated. For example, an occasional writer impugned his patriotism or complained that he spent too little time in Madison administering the University. Frank staved off the potential flood of criticism on these and similar issues by either straddling the fence or siding with what he considered to be majority opinion. Thus when a series of *Chicago Tribune* editorials accused him of taking the University down the road to pacifism, Frank spoke out against super-patriotism; and when he learned that Mrs. Bertrand Russell, wife of the English philosopher, had advocated "companionate marriage," he quickly cancelled her lecture to the University Forum on moral grounds—at the same time blandly claiming that the denial of the use of a platform did not represent an infringement upon free speech. Frank's firm action in the latter instance won him considerable praise outside the University, but it raised a doubt in the minds of many faculty members as to where he really stood on the issue of freedom of speech and inquiry. For Frank there seemed to be a gulf between theory and practice.

Nor was Frank immune to criticism from even such a long-suffering group as the Board of Visitors, whom he treated on one occasion with cavalier disregard. The Board urged him to institute far-reaching changes in the University's administrative structure; Frank replied that he was reluctant to carry out a sweeping reorganization because "in the fundamental processes of education, in the curriculum, and in teaching methods, we are due for some rather fundamental and revolutionary changes in the next 15 or 20 years."[2] To some members of the Board of Visitors these probable changes seemed all the more reason why the University should reform its administrative machinery as quickly as possible.

Whether consciously or unconsciously, Frank sought to minimize such criticism of his administration by appealing over the heads of his critics either to the University community or to the general public. As he well knew, he was at his rhetorical best in pledging his efforts to the preservation of the rights of the academician. Lucidly, he declared before an All-University Convocation assembled in the University stock pavillion on a swelteringly hot day in May, 1927: "As long as I am President of the University of Wisconsin complete and unqualified academic freedom will not only be accorded to the members of its faculties but will be vigorously defended regardless of the pressure, the power, or the prestige that may accompany any challenge of this inalienable right of scholarship."[3]

In his numerous speeches outside academe, by contrast, Frank customarily voiced the blandest of sentiments. Indeed, he seemed determined to say to each group what it wished most to hear. He told the Madison Elks Club that "The great aim in life ought to be to see in our job the best possible way to serve society." He told the Milwaukee Italian-American Club that theirs was the unfinished task of Christopher Columbus and that they had a responsibility to help "Americans Americanize Americanization." He told the Milwaukee County Medical Society that "The deep human insight of the old fashioned country doctor is needed today in the present period of highly organized scientific learning." He told a church congregation that "a prize ring can not take the place of a praying ground." He told members of the advertising profession that as merchandisers of modern thought they were carrying forward an "evangelism of science" designed to make "high-brow jargon" understandable to the masses. He told the Wisconsin Press Association that "Both the press and the University are servants of the public and depend upon the public for support." He told the Wisconsin State Bankers' Association that the greatest danger to democracy "lies in our tendencies to select leaders who are similar to the rank and file of us, whereas the hope of democracy lies in our selecting leaders who are superior to the rank and file of us." He told businessmen that they were the backbone of American life. He told laborers that they were the backbone of American life. He told farmers that they were the backbone of American life.[4]

When Frank did commit himself to a distinctive point of view, it was usually to call attention to the problems growing out of industrialization. He was consistent with his previous conclusions, though he now tended to speak out on specific issues and to offer more sweeping solutions. According to Frank, the United States was still in the midst of a period of readjustment caused by the machine age. "Until a little while ago we were conquering a continent, now we are developing an industrial civilization," he said. "And now we must somehow manage, through higher wages and shorter hours, to give men a chance for a new freedom that their forefathers found in free lands or the nation will fall victim to a sullen discontent on the part of the disinherited." Five "bloodless struggles," he contended, would have to be resolved if the nation was to meet the crisis: spiritualism versus materialism, ruralism versus urbanism, majority rule versus minority rights, decentralization versus centralization, and patriotism versus nationalism. He called for majority control of all public and private institutions, asked for complete freedom of expression, urged that new ideas be carefully examined, demanded an end to racial tensions, advocated studies to help solve technological unemployment, pleaded with big business to provide "statesmanlike administrators," suggested that materialism alone was not enough as a personal and national goal, and pressed the American people to elect intelligent representatives. In rare moments he sounded almost prophetic, as in 1928 when he declared, "Whether, during the next fifty years, our Western Civilization goes to a rendezvous with death or keeps an appointment with high destiny, will depend upon our success in bringing about a cross-fertilization between the spirituality of the East and the materialism of the West."[5]

Frank believed that the survival of the West hinged in part upon educational change. The "rigidly departmentalized college that teaches a variety of separate studies," the antiquated elective system that smacks of "an intellectual cafeteria" where "there is nothing to guide the inexperienced in his food," the college curriculums that looked like "crazy quilts," the "suicidal specialization by teachers and a suicidal smattering by students," and the tendency of colleges and universities "to become merely distributing agencies of unrelated bits of information"—all were preventing higher education from performing a necessary role in creating a democratic society. "In a modern university," Frank continued, "we are always in danger of losing that sense of intellectual and spiritual community without which the individual student may become ingrown and limited in sympathy and outlook." New methods, he contended, had to be found to carry out the main purpose of a college education—helping students to achieve the temper and techniques of the explorer, preparing them for modern society, and encouraging them to continue the learning process after graduation. The experimental college idea represented an attempt to achieve such ends, and could be expected to succeed, provided teachers could be found who thought quickly, went behind the obvious facts, engaged in ruthless self-criticism, and rejected partisan causes. "Oh, Lord of learning and learners," he intoned, "We are at best but blunderers in the God-like business of teaching. . . . We have been content to be the merchants of dead yesterday, when we should have been the guides of inborn tomorrow. . . . May we be shepherds of the spirit as well as masters of the mind."⁶

Frank never tired of delivering this and similar messages, in part because he did not sense the banality of his rhetoric, and in part, too, because he hungered both for public recognition and the financial rewards which attended it. Thus while administering a mutli-million-dollar educational institution he simultaneously advanced his career as a freelance journalist and public lecturer. He did so despite the counsel of Walter Dill Scott, president of Northwestern University. "My advice would be that you accept no invitations to write articles, and no invitations to deliver addresses that do not have to do specifically and directly with your present job," Scott had advised. "Your very great ability may lead you to overtaxing your strength. Take my advice and loaf on the job rather than write articles and make addresses on general topics."⁷ But Frank could not resist accepting some of the hundreds of invitations he received. His lecture bureau called him "A world personality of the first rank"—an outstanding educator, publicist, and speaker who charmed audiences not only because of his brilliant oratory, "but quite as much because of the new ideas he always presents and the intellectual adventuring he compels in his listeners." After Frank came to Wisconsin he increased his lecture fee from $350 to $500 an appearance, and some groups were unwilling to bear the cost. More than one program chairman wrote, "we have considerable respect for Mr. Frank's ability, but do not consider him worth $500 a lecture." Still, Frank continued to be in such demand that he averaged more than $10,000 a year from lecturing during his twelve years as president of the University of Wisconsin.⁸

He also earned another $10,000 annually from his syndicated column, which at one time appeared in seventy-nine newspapers. Their combined circulation exceeded three million readers. Frank refused to permit his column to appear in any Wisconsin newspaper, avowedly because he did not wish to seem to be favoring one newspaper in a community over another. His daily editorials, variously titled "Life's Worth Living," "Onward and Upward," "The Door Bell Speaks," "Glenn Frank's Views," and "Unconventional Views of Life," were often based on the backlog of material which he had accumulated during his years in Boston and New York and, he claimed, required only three hours of his time each week. According to the publicity distributed by the syndicate, his column inspired the downhearted, uplifted the low in spirit, and cheered the unhappy. Despite the clause in his initial employment agreement with the Board of Regents stipulating that he abandon his newspaper work, Frank signed a new contract in 1927 to continue writing his daily column. Nor did he treat lightly the work or the income it produced. In 1928 he urged his syndicate to increase circulation. "I will guarantee improved material and prompt delivery if you will promote some growth in distribution," he wrote. For several years, at least, the Board of Regents acquiesced in this and other of Frank's freelance activities.[9]

Thus Frank's income from all source averaged between $35,000 and $45,000 a year. The University furnished him with an expense account, a $90,000 home, a domestic staff, a sleek Packard sedan, and a liveried chauffeur. Still, he never seemed to have enough money on hand, and one year, incredibly, met his expenses only by borrowing $3,750 from an old friend. Frank blamed his financial troubles on the responsibilities that went with his position, contending in the late twenties that necessary and unavoidable burdens cost him almost $19,000 a year over and above his income. "I have been happy to do it," he explained, "for the problem of the State University in American development interests me enormously. I want to do a job here that I can afterward look back upon as a real contribution to my generation. I want nothing to slow up the doing of this job.[10]

A more probable explanation for Frank's financial difficulties was that he and his family lived too lavishly, both in and away from Madison. Mary Frank, who liked expensive clothes and costly jewelry, quickly established herself as the arbiter of Madison society. The presidential mansion, located in University Heights, an old and venerated residential area of the city, was the scene of brilliant parties, sometimes served by uniformed butlers and maids imported from Chicago for the occasion. Mrs. Frank held teas for students, receptions for touring farmers and their families, private dinners for the governor, dinner-dances for distinguished visitors such as Charles Lindbergh, musicales for the spouses of state legislators, bridge parties for the wives of Regents, and musicale teas for the wives of professors and businessmen. When travelling, the Franks always went first class. On their extended trips to New York City to visit old friends and see the latest Broadway productions, they often spent over a hundred dollars a day. Their son's expenses also mounted rapidly as he grew older. His parents provided him with a governess, sent him to prep school at Groton, Connecticut, and then to Harvard. The days when Glenn Frank could live on the salary of a Methodist preacher or when he and his wife could reside in Boston on a salary of even $7,500 a year were long past.[11]

All of the Franks' sybaritic tastes had to be paid for, and the president of the University often lamented the long hours of work which this required. "This joke is on me," Frank confessed. "I left the hectic haste of New York for the simple life of the middle west, and I am now looking for the man who first spoke of a 'quiet academic life.' " Likening himself to a colored slave, he claimed that he did not have a "breakfast" job, asserted that he needed a rubber calendar to stretch the days, and longed for the "sylvan stillness" of the subway. "This presidenting is a dog's life," he declared, but "I haven't yet made up my mind whether it is the life of a mongrel, a police dog, or a lap dog. It certainly offers the opportunity of intimate contact with every desirable and undesirable that goes to make a cross-section of the American social order."[12]

Frank attempted to stay far enough removed from the mass

of daily routine so that he could view the University of Wisconsin as a whole. "My judgment," he said, "is that the simpler the President's office can be kept the better." He made none of the usual appointments for administrative relief—vice president, dean of administration, or assistant to the president—because he believed that most men in such positions were liabilities rather than assets. His office staff was surprisingly small, considering the size of the University. It consisted only of himself, an executive secretary, and a stenographic secretary. Frank's aim, and it was a sensible one, was to keep the function of the president "executive" rather than "administrative." He had the Regents change the by-laws so that certain technically administrative things that a president had previously been required to do, such as signing vouchers, were turned over to the business office. This left him free to deal with major policy matters, key appointments, the "public mind" of the state, and the legislature. Under a comprehensive system of centralized control, he hoped to have coming to his desk at stated intervals brief reports giving him a continuous picture of the University's operations. These reports would give him a factual framework upon which to rest considerations of policy. He would gain a clear understanding of the problems of the University without becoming directly involved in them.[18]

Frank found that his system of administration worked so well that he was able to devote a considerable part of each working week to reading and reflecting on administrative and educational problems and trends. He arranged his office as a study rather than as a room for the reception of University officials and visitors to the campus. A large work table stood behind his desk, and on it were arranged reports, monographs, essays, and similar materials relating to his current interests. Frank regarded his reading as a critical element in his over-all grasp of his job; it played much the same function as did conferences with his staff. "I have instinctively felt that this was an intelligent use of my time," he once explained to readers of his newspaper column, "but I have always done this office reading a bit sheepishly, with a sort of half-feeling that a better executive would 'act' during office hours and 'read' in the evening."[14]

The manner in which the University had functioned historically simplified Frank's administrative tasks. In the internal operation of the institution the president exercised certain powers—such as making major appointments, formulating the budget, and dealing with the alumni—but in many other ways the University operated in a self-regulating fashion. The various deans handled many administrative details, civil service employees kept the physical plant in order and handled the necessary paperwork, the Board of Regents acted on numerous administrative and procedural matters, and faculty members helped formulate policy and decide major issues. Thus the University of Wisconsin, like any other large institution, could run a long time on the accumulated weight of bureaucratic tradition and routine, without making the president appear weak, lazy, or ineffectual. By the same token, a president who could overcome the innate inertia characteristic of such a large institution, and who could secure the enthusiastic co-operation of the administrative, teaching, and research staffs, could powerfully influence the University's development.

Perhaps the most vexing problem that Frank faced involved the formulation and adoption of the biennial budget. As he observed warily, one of his most trying tasks was "wrestling" with the University budget as it came under the legislature's extended scrutiny.[15] He was neither the first nor the last president to voice such a grievance. Luckily for the University and for his own fortunes, Frank was a masterful lobbyist. He realized that it took more than submitting a budget to the governor and more than an appearance before the all-powerful legislative joint finance committee to obtain suitable appropriations.

When the legislature was in session he went to great lengths to lay the groundwork for success. On many a winter evening, through the snow and wind, his ears tingling from the cold, he left the comforts of the presidential mansion and went down to the Madison hotels where most of the legislators made their headquarters. Frank was not a man to stand off in a corner of the lobby surreptitiously gathering assembly-men and senators around him. Rather he played the role of a "neighbor," moving from group to group, shaking hands, asking questions, telling humorous stories, discussing business conditions, never forgetting a name and seldom mentioning the University. In the grand manner, he greeted legislators with a derby in hand and a gracious bow. Throughout, he cast himself in the role of a sparkling gentleman, impartially and sincerely interested in all those gathered about him.

In due course Frank began harvesting the fruits of his assiduous labor. For several years he enjoyed the joint finance committee's sympathetic consideration of the University budget. The long evenings at the hotels had their effect, as did his dazzling presentation of the case for financial support. Unlike some previous presidents of the University, he almost invariably went alone to the committee room. He brought no statistical experts for support, and he did not tax the patience of committee members with tedious recitations of the University's needs for courses, libraries, departments, salaries, equipment, and buildings. He talked statistics, but never enough to lose the attention of his listeners, and he dramatized his data by using charts and other graphic methods of presentation. Above all, Frank used his great facility with language to paint a picture of the University's requirements—and he made it bright, sketchy, entertaining.[16]

Much advanced planning went into his presentations. Long before his actual appearance, Frank spent hours attaining an understanding of the University's past progress, present needs, and future goals. He also tried to anticipate the questions he might be called upon to answer: "Should the University be limited size?" "Can the high school inspection force of the University be limited?" "Have you any comparative figures with neighboring universities as to the teaching

cost per pupil?"[17] Sometimes, when the budget seemed hope-
lessly bogged down in committee, Frank wondered if it were
all worthwhile. "The tussle with the legislative Finance
Committee has this year shown striking resemblance to the
outdoor sport of beating one's head against a stone wall, but,
as the poet puts it, our head is bloody but unbowed, and
light is beginning to filter through cracks that are beginning
to appear here and there in the wall," he observed ruefully
in 1929. "Happily, hope springs eternal in the breast of even
the most respectable lobbyist."[18] While he did not always
receive everything that he asked for, Frank's advance prepara-
tions paid handsome dividends; legislative appropriations
increased by over twenty per cent during the first four years of
his administration. As a veteran legislator commented,
"When Dr. Frank tells his story the boys want to throw money
at him in $100,000 lots."[19]

In his first budget request, Frank obtained the funds needed to begin the Experimental College. The "X College,"
under the directorship of Alexander Meiklejohn, opened
in September, 1927, and functioned until June, 1932. It
began with 119 students and closed with 66. The "guinea
pigs" and their "advisers" lived together in Adams Hall, one
of the larger University dormitories. Both the two-year curriculum and the teaching methods of the Experimental College differed radically from the rest of the University. The
freshman year was devoted to a survey of the Athens of Plato
and Pericles, and the sophomore year to a study of nineteenth-
and twentieth-century American civilization. By studying
"situations rather than subjects" and a single dominant
"scheme of reference," students were expected to achieve
"organic growth and development." Aside from a compul-
sory lecture on Monday mornings, students worked at their
own pace. They read massive amounts of material, compiled
comprehensive regional surveys of their home towns or districts, and made oral and written reports on Athenian and
Spartan mores, the role of the middleman in society, and
the problems currently facing the federal government. In

addition, they received guidance through conferences with their advisers "of such a frequency and kind that the teacher can have real acquaintance with the mind of his pupil," and through intensive group discussions that constituted "talks rather than lectures." The advisers gave no formal grades, but after students completed the program they were "promoted" to the University proper with an alphabetical grade. Frank, recalling his own educational experiences in Northwestern University, told an Experimental College class that the curriculum made him jealous with "low browed, green-eyed, unchristian envy."[20]

The College proved a mixed blessing for the Frank administration. On the one hand, it attracted favorable comment throughout the nation, helped along by frequent references in Frank's column and by Meiklejohn's articles in various national publications. The governor of New York, Franklin D. Roosevelt, even considered enrolling his son Elliot in the program. On the other hand, the College encountered so many difficulties that Meiklejohn soon wished that the experiment had been entirely separate from the University proper. In 1932 he wrote, "The college from the beginning was involved in strains and conflicts destructive of its healthy and normal development."[21]

A variety of unhappy circumstances plagued the Experimental College during its five-year existence. Many students ridiculed the owl—"the bird of Athens"—embroidered on blazers which the Experimental College students wore, looked with displeasure on the large number of Jews and out-of-staters enrolled in the College, and denounced the lack of formal examinations. Inevitably, a few people said that the "X College" harbored communists. A letter in the *Wisconsin State Journal* charged that a fictitious "Professor Pinkevitch" had compared the experiment to educational projects in the Soviet Union, while a self-styled authority on Marxism interviewed by the *Chicago Tribune* hinted that some of the theories expounded in the College came "devilishly close to Bolshevism." The officials of the Experimental

College did little to quiet such critics. Bravely ignoring public opinion, they readmitted a Russian Jew from New York City after he had served a jail sentence for reciting an obscene poem about capitalism before a Young Communist League meeting. Inside the College cleavages occurred between Jews and gentiles, between radicals and conservatives, and between fraternity and non-fraternity men. Most of these difficulties ironed themselves out, as did complaints about the students' "boorish and uncouth" table manners. Still, in the end, very few students from Wisconsin remained in the program.[22]

Academic advisers in the College encountered serious difficulties of another sort. They held regular faculty appointments and were expected to spend a third of their time instructing in courses outside the College. Most of them owed their appointments to Meiklejohn's influence, but in matters of tenure, promotion, and salary they were at the mercy of the various Bascom Hill departments. In many instances "regular" departmental members looked upon them as interlopers and disdained the experiment. One adviser said that he constantly faced faculty hostility, and especially a "negative and narrow conception of classical study." Several advisers successfully walked the tightrope between these conflicting interests. They secured permanent appointments following the demise of the Experimental College, and several of them went on to become leading authorities in their respective fields. But many others resigned after spending only a year or two in the College, and still others left Madison when the experiment was abandoned.[23]

The College also suffered from Meiklejohn's lack of concern with administrative detail. He was especially lax in distributing material to parents and prospective students, even after Frank had warned him in 1928, "Unless some of you in the College take the matter in hand, next year may be very embarrassing and see the whole experiment jeopardized."[24] For his part, Frank hurt the project's fortunes from its very inception by failing to make at least a show of soliciting the views of older faculty members—who were very conscious of their prerogatives. Apparently, he felt that his often repeated desire to consult with the faculty on basic issues had been fulfilled when it voted in favor of the scheme. Moreover, in many of his speeches praising the experiment he caused ill-feeling among the teaching staff by dwelling on the need to overcome the shortsighted thinking of tradition-bound educators.

Faculty resentment gradually smoldered, finally flaring into the open on March 8, 1929, when Dean George Sellery of the College of Letters and Science criticized the Experimental College in an address before a Freshmen Convocation. He praised the contributions of the "regular" faculty and charged that the "X College" had failed to achieve its overall purpose. He asserted that the dormitory system hampered individuality, that freshmen and sophomores were unprepared for such an advanced approach, that an entire civilization could not be adequately covered in a single academic year, and that students received inadequate training in scientific matters.[25] Two days later Sellery, whose office was only a few steps from Frank's, sent the president a letter explaining his criticism. Sellery said, "My purpose was to say some kind, encouraging and deserved things about the alumni and faculty of the College of Letters and Science at large and to give their recent critics the salutary even if novel experience of a little taste of their own medicine. For there should not be the slightest doubt of this: many strong members of the faculty have been hurt and their efficiency impaired by the intermittent, long-range condemnation which it has had to endure for a year or so. The faculty is fully conscious of the great desirability of improving the situation. In telling University and teacher audiences here and there over the country that Liberal Arts faculties—and that is understood to mean our faculty in the first instance—are mossback or even worse— a disservice has been done. . . . The outcry which my address provoked in some quarters—and probably more will be forthcoming—shows, to my great satisfaction, that there is now a fuller appreciation of the desirability of tolerance and fine words."[28] With these blunt words, Glenn Frank was drawn short, caught completely unawares. Clearly, he had misjudged his position and had not prepared his ground for the seed of new experimental ideas.

Sellery's actions marked the end of the first phase of Frank's administration. Soon, for reasons which Frank never fully understood, other critics, even more powerful, would come forward. Frank stood at the brink of several years of turmoil. The great impersonal economic forces of the Depression would harshly grip his attention. As never before, he would be tested as a person and as an administrator.

VIII

On Trial

BY 1930 THE UNIVERSITY OF WISCONSIN had reached a crossroad. It could either continue to develop along the path it had followed over the preceding generation, or it could strike out in one of several new directions. However, the University's freedom of action was constrained by political pressures, charges of faculty incompetence, internal discontent, and dissension over the proper lines of educational experimentation. Too, the Great Depression was already casting an ominous shadow over University affairs, and no one could predict how intense the state's economic difficulties would become or how long the crisis would last.

Glenn Frank also stood at a crossroad. Over the previous five years, from 1925 to 1930, he had been motivated by one overriding goal—to build a solid basis of good will within the University, the legislature, and the state. On the whole he had succeeded. His congenial personality, his efforts to avoid controversy, his willingness to delegate authority, and his determination to keep on good terms with everyone had gradually built up for him a fund of mutual respect, even admiration. Intuitively, Frank had sought to insure himself against the day when a crisis threatened.

But how securely Frank had built remained an unknown factor in the equation. His success had come during a period of unusual tranquility in the University's history; the legislature had not felt obliged by economic pressures

104

to deal parsimoniously with his budget requests, the Progressives had shown little inclination to question his devotion to the "Wisconsin Idea," and there had been no divisive crisis to test his administrative skills. True, there was growing opposition to the Experimental College, but educational change seldom pleases everyone and even George Sellery, the most outspoken critic of the project, seemed anxious to avoid a showdown. Yet, with the advantage of hindsight, it is now clear that Frank's capacity to lead the University through an impending round of crises was about to be tested. Would his methods of administration prove equal to the demands that would be made upon them? Or would the University's problems call for an entirely different kind of leader, one willing to take controversial stands and, if necessary, to deal firmly with those who opposed or obstructed his policies? To date Frank had shown little inclination to be such a president.

The days ahead would determine if Frank had pursued the right course between 1925 and 1930. He would find out if by giving parties and making innocuous speeches he had insured himself against times of controversy. Events would show whether he should have been building support of a fundamentally different character. In other words—in his dealings with professors, deans, legislators, governors, alumni, regents, and citizens—had he cultivated the right kinds of loyalties? When people applauded, were they cheering him and his policies or what he represented as president of the University of Wisconsin? Was there any positive commitment to the man himself and to his program?

The conditions brought on by the Depression created an atmosphere within academe which inflated minor crises and petty squabbles into potentially dangerous incidents, incidents which caused Frank far more difficulty than would have been the case in less troubled times. On the surface, of course, and to the general public, the University functioned much as it had always done; but in reality the faculty and the deans increasingly made decisions which would normally have been made by the president himself. And beneath the surface, where change was less easy to observe except by people close to the institution, the University was undergoing significant changes which were gradually though imperceptibly transforming its role in the life of the state.

During the early 1930's a School of Education finally became a reality, graduate school officials enacted major internal reforms, and the programs of the Extension Division and the School of Agriculture were broadened in scope. Then, too, the Wisconsin Alumni Research Foundation (WARF) became an important arm of the University, a freshman orientation program went into operation, the functions of some of the deans underwent major changes, and the business office was reorganized. Frank naturally claimed credit for these developments. He did this through press releases and in the pages of the *Wisconsin Alumni Magazine*. Actually, his role was confined to making a few proposals and to issuing broad statements of policy. Aside from the Experimental College, most of the changes he recommended had been under consideration for several years, and he never liked to participate directly in formulating the details of programs.

The students were the first to feel the effects of the Depression. The relaxed "normalcy" of the 1920's—where the main topics of discussion were the use of "king nicotine," the annual all-school prom, the financing of new fraternity and sorority houses, the kinds of clothes a flapper should have in her wardrobe, the number of people who belonged to the "Circle of the Godless," the extent of drinking among co-eds, and the usual worries over term papers and examinations—gave gave way to an entirely different situation. Frank's initial prediction that the Depression would "speed up" enrollment failed to be borne out and the number of students declined from 8,500 in 1929 to 7,000 in 1932. For a while student jobs seemed nonexistent; some students reportedly lived on less than fifty cents a day.[1]

The economic collapse gradually affected other aspects of

the University's operation. In 1931, the legislature drastically reduced the budget for higher education. This halted the University's building program. Several new structures, including dormitories, the University Hospital, the field house, and the Memorial Union, had been completed before work was stopped, and the football stadium had been enlarged. But a badly needed new library remained on the drawing boards—not to be constructed until the 1950's. The financial crisis also forced the Experimental College to close in 1932, and its dean, Alexander Meiklejohn, went on an extended leave of absence. He left behind him a project which had never fulfilled the high hopes that Frank had envisioned for it. The economies forced on the University administration bore especially heavily upon the faculty. Except for the sciences, research grants were almost impossible to obtain. This forced most members of the faculty to look to teaching rather than to research for support. But to live within its means, and to provide salaries for permanent staff members, the administration cut back on appointments by not replacing men who retired or resigned, by sharply increasing the instructional load, and, in the case of undergraduate discussion sections, by replacing postgraduate assistants with professors. Other economies, such as removing telephones from faculty offices, were also put into effect.[2]

On July 1, 1932, the Board of Regents—with the reluctant help and approval of the faculty—instituted a complicated and unpopular series of salary cuts euphemistically called "waivers." They ranged from an average of twelve per cent for teaching and research assistants to twenty per cent for full professors. Since the salary scale had ranged from six thousand to ten thousand dollars a year, the reductions imposed on the younger faculty members, though proportionately smaller than those imposed on their elders, nevertheless bore especially heavily upon them.

The faculty committee which had formulated the mechanical details of the waiver system had assumed that President Frank would impose comparable reductions on the administrative staff, including himself. Instead, he persuaded the Regents that a maximum reduction of twenty per cent would be adequate. So his salary of $20,400 was cut accordingly, but the reduction was far less than the twenty-five to thirty per cent which most faculty members expected him to take. Moreover, he did not adjust his presidential fringe benefits, but continued to live in his accustomed lavish style.

Dissatisfaction among the small group which knew about the budget rose quickly and as soon as the size of Frank's waiver became common knowledge on the campus his popularity plummeted. By this one thoughtless act he contributed immeasurably to the ill-will which was gradually building up against him. It was probably the most unpopular and long-remembered action of his entire administration. The widespread dissatisfaction was compounded several months later when the University purchased a new automobile for his use—a $3,500 Lincoln Continental—and continued to provide him with a liveried chauffeur. Thereafter, Glenn Frank was to find it increasingly difficult to secure the ready co-operation of his faculty and staff.[3]

At much the same time, various other internal crises further impaired Frank's effectiveness as an administrator. The first and most flamboyant of these was dubbed the "Rocking Chair Scandal." It occurred shortly before the Christmas vacation of 1929 and involved the Dean of Men, Scott Goodnight, the Dean of Women, F. Louise Nardin, and a professor of English, William Ellery Leonard, who also enjoyed a modest reputation as a poet. It raised some fundamental questions about the extent and nature of the University's obligation to oversee the private affairs of its students.

The incident started as a routine disciplinary matter. Around eight o'clock on Saturday morning, December 16, Dean Nardin called Dean Goodnight out of a conference and asked him to investigate the second story of an apartment building near the campus. Goodnight considered the call routine. He and Dean Nardin handled all discipline within the University and they were accustomed to working together. Goodnight hurried to the apartment, expecting to find either an all-night drinking party or a case of exhibitionism from a window. When he arrived the person who answered the door invited him to enter the apartment. Once inside, Goodnight realized that a co-ed and a male student were together on a locked sleeping-porch. "I heard whisperings and then the truth of the situation came to me," he reported. The dean waited until the couple came out, obtained their names, and then left. As he recalled, he was back in his office by nine o'clock. Early the following week, in keeping with University regulations, he used his disciplinary powers to expel the male student; Dean Nardin expelled the girl.[4]

That would have ended the affair, had not Professor Leonard intervened. On January 9, 1930, he wrote to Frank that "There occurred about two weeks before Christmas, an episode, which, when it came to my ears, aroused in me such amazement and doubts that I turned from my leisurely and remote Greek and Latin studies in Plato and Epicurus and Lucretius on the conduct of life to an intensive study of a special problem of conduct in the very modern and specific world at the University of Wisconsin, as revealed in the conduct of Dr. S. H. Goodnight our Dean of Men." Leonard charged that the "foxy" dean had with "righteous and peremptory vigor" illegally invaded the apartment, heard noises on the locked sleeping-porch, called police when the door remained closed, and then waited patiently in a rocking chair for their arrival. Leonard argued that the couple were fully clothed and that "free love" was not involved in the incident because "one knows the quiet secret that on that particular night the woman was under the Law of Diana, and not of Aphrodite, and was there simply to be near the man she loved."[5]

Leonard was considered by many observers to be an eccentric who thrived on controversy. In 1927, in his autobiography, *The Locomotive God,* he had recounted how he had gradually developed a horrible phobia following his mother's death in an insane asylum, his first wife's suicide, and his "social ostracism" from Madison society. As a consequence of his affliction, he said that whenever he journeyed more than a few blocks from his apartment "prison" near the University campus, he cringed in fear and fell on the ground in a convulsive fit. He had written that he was "in as fierce a panic of isolation, from help and home and in as great a dread of immediate death as a man high in a skyscraper with the flames lapping his shoulders." He traced his fear to his third birthday when a locomotive had terrified him.[6]

Frank would have been well-advised to have taken some action on Leonard's letter, either by conducting an investigation of the charges or by calling a conference of the interested parties. But that was not his style. Instead he chose to ignore the letter. Offended by the president's apparent rebuff, Leonard released his letter to the newspapers. Nothing could have been better calculated to embarrass the University. The "Rocking Chair Scandal" was immediately headlined in newspapers throughout the state. The wire services picked up the story and readers all over the country were soon savoring the apparently sordid details of a campus scandal.

On the whole, editorial writers and alumni sided with Frank rather than Leonard. "Prof. Leonard should be unceremoniously fired," declared the editor of the *Merrill Daily Herald*. "So long as the University of Wisconsin employs men with the ideas of W. E. Leonard and the desire to broadcast them," wrote an irate alumnus, "I feel it is not a safe place for boys and girls."[7]

With a particularly sensitive area of University affairs thus exposed to public gaze, Frank should have acted vigorously and quickly to repair the damage that his initial indifference to Leonard's charges had caused. Instead, he hurried off to Georgia on a lucrative lecture tour without so much as issuing a statement designed to reassure the public, let alone instituting an administrative investigation. Perhaps he believed that the public outcry would subside of its own accord and that any statement he might make would only exacerbate feelings throughout the state. Nevertheless, his handling of the scandal looked incompetent and indecisive, the more so when Leonard declared that he would never have released the letter to the press if Frank had asked him to withhold it for the good of the University.[8]

Over the long haul, however, the incident did lead to positive action, though by the faculty rather than the administration. The faculty first reviewed the functions of the deans of men and women, and then, on May 1, 1931, voted to transfer disciplinary matters from the deans to a new faculty committee on student misconduct.

Frank failed to use this opportunity to institute fundamental changes in the relations between the University and its student body. On the contrary, he made Dean Nardin the scapegoat for the incident, undermined Dean Goodnight's influence, and continued to emphasize the public relations aspect of disciplinary problems. He removed Dean Nardin from office at the first opportunity, arguing that stories about her, "publicized and blown up as a result of the rocking chair case," had impaired her usefulness. There may have been some truth in this interpretation. Certainly, the mother of the expelled girl declared, "Dean Nardin was perfectly cruel, cold, and heartless toward her innocent victim." But Frank may have used the incident to rid himself of a dean whom he personally disliked. Goodnight, who retained his deanship, approved of the transfer of disciplinary matters to a faculty committee. However, he defended his conduct and insisted, "It is simply not true that we are tyrants or despots." Nevertheless, he lost favor with Frank, who directed the newly appointed discipline committee to act circumspectly. "The important thing," wrote Frank, "is to get the consideration of the few cases that come up in the course of a year out of the spotlight so that the damnably morbid interest that has heretofore been centered on 'discipline' will be broken and the atmosphere normalized and made healthier.

I can see no necessity for any one's padding about town as a police investigator.'"[9]

The committee proceeded as Frank desired, devoting most of its efforts to producing long reports on the conditions which created discipline problems. It instituted no major changes in policy, although it did manage to keep cases that came before it out of the public spotlight. No further rocking chair scandals occurred.

Frank later explained that he did not enter the public controversy over the incident because he had expressed his opinion by confirming the expulsion of the two students. He did not mention that he had failed to support members of his own administration, that he had allowed a professor without jurisdiction to interefere in a manner which had damaged the University's reputation, that he had taken steps to change the discipline machinery only after the damage had been done, and that in the eyes of the Regents part of his function was to prevent such controversies from occurring.

A few years later, in 1935, two other scandals rocked the University of Wisconsin. The first involved the Extension Divisions, the second the Department of Athletics. The Extension scandal centered around Chester D. Snell, who had been director of the Division since 1926. People considered him a Frank appointee and noted that the two men found much to admire in each other. Young, tall, and broad-shouldered, with a ready smile and a faint Southern accent, Snell had previously directed the extension program of the University of North Carolina. An administrator rather than scholar, he had summed up his weaknesses when he informed Frank, "There is a side to me which you have not seen—when running in high gear I am quite an autocrat and driver—you know that it takes time to build an efficient organization in a short period. . . ." Almost from the moment he arrived in Madison, Snell had gained a reputation as an "empire builder," and his aggressive policies, often pursued tactlessly, soon aroused enmities. He talked about the incompetence of subordinates and ridiculed past policies. Within a few years he had replaced six of fourteen major administrators in the Division. He had told Frank, "I admit that a rather complete 'wrecking' job was done, but I do not think there are many people who will say this interfered with the regular program; in fact, I think conditions began to improve from the start."

Snell's critics admitted that he had added some able men and had initiated needed curriculum and administrative reforms in a division that for many years had been living on a reputation made twenty-five years earlier. But they attacked his lack of tact, frequent firings, and drive to extend his authority. More than once he had ignored advice to proceed more slowly. As his general unpopularity grew over the years—he alienated most of the other deans by tampering in their areas of jurisdiction—his downfall seemed only a matter of time. The climax came in the spring of 1935, when Snell tried to establish closer control over the Extension Center in Milwaukee. He made unpopular removals, then alleged that certain members of the Milwaukee faculty who opposed him had attended a series of immoral drinking parties on a yacht in Lake Michigan.

The Board of Regents investigated these charges. After holding closed hearings they concluded that Snell was no longer capable of making policy, that he was dictatorial and unethical toward his subordinates, that he was guilty of poor sportsmanship in his relations with others, and that he was unfitted by education—like Frank he had only a bachelor's degree—for the job he had performed for nine years. In April, 1935, the Regents asked Snell to resign. When he refused, they voted unanimously to remove him from office. Snell was the first major University official to be removed in the twentieth century, a fact which reflected the Regents' growing disenchantment with Frank himself. And, as events unfolded, Snell proved to be only the first of several important administrators who were forced to resign.[10]

In December, 1935, a controversy in the Department of

Athletics, only nominally controlled by the faculty, prompted the Regents to conduct another investigation. The principal figures were the athletic director, Walter Meanwell, renowned for having coached the basketball team to numerous championships, and Clarence Spears, the football coach since 1932. By coincidence, both men were medical doctors. Spears, a man of great bulk, had a nationwide reputation for "toughness." He had said, "Football isn't a lackadaisical game. You can't play it that way. If you're going to play football, you might as well play to win." The University Athletic Board—eager in the face of alumni pressure to obtain a winning coach—had hired Spears despite the knowledge that he had caused embarrassment to several other schools by losing his temper in public. A man who knew him well had said, "If we could let him do the coaching and then lock him in the closet until practice the next day, we'd get along better." Among other things, at the University of Wisconsin, Spears came under fire for driving his players, shoving a photographer aside to obtain a better view of a game, and producing a dismal series of losing teams.[11]

But this was merely prelude. The investigation concerned a different set of circumstances. The Regents wanted to know if Spears and Meanwell were engaged in a struggle for control of the athletic department; if Spears had used his medical standing to secure the release of seriously injured players from the student infirmary so they could play in games; if Spears had ordered a trainer to give the team brandy at half-time to stimulate their efforts in the last two quarters; and if Meanwell had profited from a business connection with a company from which the University bought football equipment. Spears and Meanwell denied the charges, but after hearing lengthy testimony the Regents concluded that the allegations were true and fired both men. As an aftermath, and at the urging of the commissioner of the conference to which the University of Wisconsin belonged, the Regents allowed the faculty to assume closer control over athletics.[12]

Frank's roles in the Extension and athletic investigations

further hurt his reputation as an administrator. In the Snell matter Frank tried to strengthen his position by letting it be known that he had urged the Regents to dismiss the director. Many faculty members endorsed the removal but questioned Frank's motives, the more so when it became known that Frank had given Snell a favorable recommendation for a position at another institution. Frank said that Snell possessed "genuine ability and force." Snell was not grateful and claimed that Frank had "winked" at immorality, failed to support his own policies, suppressed evidence, and hurt the University by "prancing" around the country making speeches. Frank refused to support either Spears or Meanwell, although both had obtained their positions under his presidency. While the hearings were underway Frank said, "As long as I am engaged in this investigation I shall voice no opinion." Afterwards he stated, "For the last four years the administration of athletics at the university has been made increasingly difficult by the fact that so many outside forces insisted upon intervening. At the end of the recent controversy it was possible for the first time to deal with the athletic problem exactly as we deal with other problems of policy and personnel at the university. I hope that some will be impressed by the fact that as soon as the administration of athletics was placed on the same basis as the administration of other parts of the University a prompt, peaceful, and generally satisfactory solution was reached." Many people—including the president of the Board of Regents and the governor of Wisconsin—wondered why Frank had not acted to reform the department sooner and on his own initiative. They voiced the same doubts about Frank's handling of the Snell affair.[18]

Besides these problems, Frank had to contend with charges that the University was a hotbed of sedition and communism. What passed for radicalism inside the University involved a small, vocal group of students. They joined such organizations as the League for Industrial Democracy, the Young Communist League, and the National Student League; delivered May Day addresses before small groups of jeering

fellow students; led protest demonstrations against the Re-
serve Officer's Training Corps; sang *America the Beautiful*
instead of the *Star Spangled Banner* because they wanted
to avoid singing about rockets' red glare and bombs burst-
ing in air; read poems condemning the bourgeoisie; and
sent supplies to striking miners in Kentucky.

These activities neither threatened the government of the
United States nor reflected the sentiment of the overwhelming majority of students. Yet the presence of the young radicals on campus brought the University under more than normal pressure, some of which may have reflected a combination of anti-semitic and anti-Eastern prejudice. It was commonly charged that the leading "radicals" came from New
York and that they had "Jewish" names. Such allegations were
without factual foundation. Nor was it even true that large
numbers of New York Jews attended the University. Nevertheless, in the early 1930's newspaper accounts of "leftish"
activities stimulated an increasing flow of protest letters into
Frank's office. Many correspondents singled out the Experimental College for particular criticism. Others urged
Frank to cleanse the University of communist influence. One
of the more extreme critics said, "TEAR DOWN THE RED FLAG
AND LET THE STARS AND STRIPES WAVE OVER AN AMERICAN UNI-
VERSITY."[14] Correspondents of this type, while a nuisance,
posed no threat to either Frank or the University, but political leaders who echoed their charges were another matter.

Several men attempted to gain political advantage in Wisconsin in the 1930's by exploiting the anti-communist issue.
Among them was John Chapple, a newspaper publisher from
Ashland, Wisconsin. In the middle 1920's he had written
glowing accounts of life in the Soviet Union. For a time he
had dabbled in Democratic and Progressive politics, but in
the early 1930's he became an orthodox Republican and an
outspoken anti-communist. His book, *La Follette Socialism,*
published in 1930, assailed the La Follettes and the University,
and impugned Frank's patriotism. Chapple charged that the
"President of our state university casts reflections upon the

American system, declares it to be challenged by communism and thinks more about the welfare of the masses than we do." In the early months of 1932, Chapple stumped the state denouncing both Frank and the University. He accused Frank of belonging to "Communist Defending" organizations, ridiculed him as a "soap-box orator with his face washed," asserted that numerous professors were disloyal to the United States, claimed that atheism flourished on the campus, and hinted that many faculty members and students practiced "free love." Basing his campaign for elective office on his opposition to communism, Chapple soon became a candidate for the Republican nomination for the United States Senate. Chapple won a startling victory in the 1932 Republican primary, but suffered a crushing defeat in the general election. He attributed his loss to the Franklin D. Roosevelt landslide and never again sought elective office. From time to time, however, he renewed his charges against the University and in 1935 he published another book about disloyalty among administrators, professors, and students. But by that time few people paid much attention to him. Nevertheless his use of the communist issue was not entirely lost upon other aspiring politicians. It was probably no coincidence that almost two decades later a United States Senator from Wisconsin hurled somewhat similar charges of communist infiltration at the United States Department of State.[15]

In the spring of 1935, State Senator William Burnette, a Republican from Green Bay, conducted a legislative investigation of radicalism in the University. Apparently he believed Chapple's charges to be well founded. The legislature, though doubting the need for or wisdom of an investigation, sanctioned it out of fear of being considered apathetic about the "communist menace," but limited its scope by refusing to appropriate funds for a professional investigator. This did not stop Burnette. He conducted open hearings at which he and his committee, called the "Red Raiders" by the press, fared badly in heated exchanges with various faculty members. He also studied syndicalist laws passed by other states, and made numerous visits to the campus, where he kept detailed notes of what he saw. He commented that "anyone reading bulletins in Entrance Hall would believe that he had entered a Communist institution." In addition, Burnette compiled dossiers on all students suspected of radicalism. These files contained such annotations as "leader in Young Communist League . . . one of the original organizers . . . and active leader in Communist Party . . . active in appearing on its programs, committees, etc." Burnette also copied information from a membership blank which stated, "THE YOUNG COMMUNIST LEAGUE fights for the replacement of capitalism by a system *truly* representative of the American people." At various times he attended meetings of the National Student League. At one meeting he listened to a small group of students sing—probably for his benefit— *I'm Labor* ("I clear the tracks so the trains can go. But someone else gets all the dough. I'm Labor") ; *Whirlwinds of Danger* ("Still in the fight see advancing before us Red Flag of Labor that yet shall prevail") ; and a little-known version of *Casey Jones* ("Casey Jones, get busy shoveling sulphur. That's what you get for scabbing on the S. P. Line") .[16]

Somewhat unexpectedly, Burnette concluded that communism was not running rampant on the campus of the University of Wisconsin. He admitted privately, even while the investigation was in progress, that 99.5 per cent of the students were loyal to the United States and that his sense of decency was offended by some of the scurrilous letters he received asserting the contrary view. His own observations, which were reinforced by pressure from Republican alumni who threatened him with political oblivion and from newspaper editors who ridiculed his efforts, helped him make up his mind that Chapple's allegations were unfounded. Nevertheless, he tried to save face by chiding Frank for "laxity" and by concluding his formal report to the Senate with a sweeping condemnation: "This committee found that for several years past the university was being advertised extensively both in this state and throughout the nation as an ultra-liberal institution and one in which communistic teachings were encouraged and avowed communists were welcome upon the campus with the permission and connivance of the administration of the university—its officers and regents. The committee investigated these reports and found they were true to the extent that they were a matter of common knowledge."[77] Although Burnette's report contained no recommendations, and although he then abandoned his harassment of the University, the investigation had subjected the institution to ridicule without at the same time reassuring the public that all was well on the campus.

During the Burnette investigation an incident occurred which members of the University community regarded as a serious threat to academic freedom. On the evening of May 15, 1935, an organizer addressed a meeting of the League for Industrial Democracy in a Law School classroom on "The Crisis on the Coast—a Preview of American Fascism." The gathering began quietly with approximately twenty men and women students present, but it was soon disrupted by the arrival of almost two hundred more, including some athletes. These young men were wearing their letter sweaters. They called themselves the "Silver Shirts," and constituted a self-appointed campus vigilante organization. The now crowded meeting grew steadily more disorderly until finally a riot broke out. In the pandemonium, someone cried, "Into the lake with the radicals!" The "Silver Shirts" seized the speaker and some of his most ardent supporters, dragged and carried them from the Law School building to nearby Lake Mendota, and, ignoring protests that their conduct was "a disgrace to the 'W' you wear on your breast," threw them into the lake. A large crowd, which included several Madison policemen, watched and cheered. The only casualty was an athlete who called one of the co-eds a "dirty Jew." The girl struck him across the mouth, knocking out one of his teeth.

The incident caused much excitement, and its meaning was hotly debated throughout the state. A Madison clergyman charged in a radio address that anti-semitism had sparked the rioting, newspapers editorialized against radicalism or in favor of free speech, and University officials received hundreds of letters either lauding the rioters or protesting the supposed attack on freedom of discussion.

As soon as Frank heard about the riot he issued a statement denouncing the "Silver Shirts." He also acted on his own authority to call a special convocation. On the oppressively hot and humid evening of May 17, 1935, over a thousand students, faculty, and townspeople crowded the auditorium and entrances of Agriculture Hall to hear Frank and ten other University leaders, including Dean George Sellery, uphold the right of students to free discussion. Frank declared that the safety and progress of the nation demanded that the minority be heard. "If a man's grievance is just," he argued, "we should hear him, and straightway correct the injustice. If a man's grievance is imaginary we should hear him, and then pit our brains against his to prove that his grievance is imaginary. To deny him a hearing is not to protect the republic. On the contrary, it is the one sure way to convince him that force or violence is the only language left to him."

Frank also dealt directly with the 147 known participants in the riot. He threatened them with expulsion from the University unless they publicly apologized for their behavior. They did so in a statement issued to the press a week later. No further action was necessary. Some faculty members criticized Frank for going over the head of the committee on student misconduct, but Dean Sellery disagreed. He noted that Frank had no choice because the committee had failed to act. Others close to University affairs believed that Frank's handling of the incident had prevented serious trouble. He had dealt swiftly with a potentially dangerous outburst of lawlessness. His effort was all the more commendable in view of the apparent reluctance of the Madison police to maintain law and order.[18]

Frank's defense of academic freedom was in keeping with his own strongly held views and with the tradition of the

University. He never hesitated to use the full power and influence of his office to check what he regarded as the dangerous activities of the Chapples and the Burnettes of the state. At the Senior-Alumni Banquet in June, 1932, for example—held at the time when Chapple's influence seemed greatest—Frank declared, "The University must never become a docile house-organ for the Stalwarts, Progressives, Socialists, or what have you. The car of progress is not a well oiled machine rolling down hill. It is a car chugging uphill and takes all that intelligent men and women can do to push it. I appeal to the traditional intelligence of the sons and daughters of the University not to surrender to any trumped up hysteria." Frank dealt even more harshly with Burnette. He publicly defended the right of professors to report their findings without fear of intimidation, sent a letter to the parents of every student in which he declared that the University administration would never turn its back on freedom of speech, and induced the leaders of the alumni association to apply behind-the-scene pressure to Burnette to modify his views. In addition, he protested to the president of the alumni association that the Burnette investigation "persists in going its own way as a committee of prosecution rather than as a committee of investigation."[19]

While stoutly defending the University and its tradition of academic freedom, Frank also resolutely opposed Marxist ideology. "I cannot conceive a more tragic fate for my country," he declared, "than its infection by the Communist philosophy." Nevertheless, he believed that communists and other people holding unpopular views had a right to express their ideas. For Frank supported complete freedom of discussion, arguing that "just as a germ dies in the sunlight, but thrives in the fetid air of a dungeon, so radical ideas are less dangerous when expressed than when repressed." He also contended that "latter-day witch-burners" ruined their cause by "aping" fascist and communist methods.[20]

When not busy reacting to these crises, Frank administered the University in much the same manner as he had since taking office. He advocated educational changes, made administrative appointments, kept himself in the public eye, and so far as possible, stood clear of the day-to-day operations of the University. He was at his best before audiences and spoke to state groups as often as he could. In one thirty-day period he addressed alumni associations in seven different cities. At such gatherings he carefully cultivated the leading business and professional men in the community, and usually called for educational programs calculated to carry forward the "Wisconsin Idea." He also urged the faculty to consider the production of educational movies and the establishment of a laboratory to help business and industry. Sometimes he spoke vaguely of forming the University's departments into what he described as a "Functional Organization of Faculty Forces." Faculty committees considered these ideas, but abandoned their discussions when Frank himself showed little interest in pursuing the proposals. Over the years, Frank also had several opportunities to fill key administrative positions. Many of his appointees proved good choices and they served the University with distinction. But in several instances he failed to follow up the tentative approaches which he had made to prospective candidates and it took him almost two years to appoint a dean for the Law School. All of these appointees, of course, considered their allegiance to be to the University rather than to the president, and without exception none of them publicly supported Frank as the criticism of his administration increased. By that time Frank had few supporters left within the University.[21]

On one occasion, Frank acted out of character. Early in 1932, he decided to remove Sellery as dean of the College of Letters and Science. However, he had barely begun to carry out this delicate and potentially dangerous maneuver when he realized that the dean had too much power to be dislodged without a struggle. Frank, who was by nature not the man to force such an issue, immediately reversed his decision and quietly dropped the matter. Unfortunately, Frank had shown his hand, and although Sellery heard only vague whispers of the president's intentions, relations between the two deteriorated still further. Too late, Frank realized that he had committed a major tactical error; he had lost the support of even a doubtful ally.[22]

Frank might have succeeded in ousting Sellery had he retained Philip Fox La Follette's good will. The slightly built second son of "Fighting Bob" La Follette was elected governor in 1930 as a Progressive Republican, was defeated in the election of 1932, then returned to office in 1934 as the gubernatorial candidate of his own Wisconsin Progressive party. On the surface Frank had maintained good relations with the La Follette family. Indeed, he had gone out of his way to gain its support. At a memorial service for the Senator in 1927, for example, he had prayed: "Almighty God, Lord alike of the leaders and the led, sacrament of remembrance, bathe our spirits in the beneficial memory of a leader who in life stood with his back to the past and in death fell his face toward the future." Frank particularly extolled the elder La Follette's contribution to the University. "He brought to its problems," Frank said, "a statesmanlike vision of a State University as an indispensable instrument of the modern state for the economic betterment, the intellectual stimulation, and the spiritual enrichment of the lives of its citizens." At first, Philip La Follette believed that Frank was going to be a successful president. "One of the things we need is that personal touch—that warmth of human personality that I feel you are going to spread," he had written Frank in 1927. However, he began to have doubts during the next two years when he served as a part-time lecturer on the law faculty. By the time that he assumed the governorship for the first time, in 1930, he had become critical of the way that Frank had used money appropriated by the legislature and he was disturbed that what he called "dead wood" remained on the faculty.[23]

La Follette's growing disenchantment with Frank was stimulated by a shift in the attitude of Theodore Kronshage, the president of the Board of Regents at the time of Frank's

selection. Kronshage had been a very close friend and adviser of "Old Bob." Philip La Follette, like his father, respected Kronshage and valued his advice. A few years before his death in 1931, Kronshage concluded that Frank
lacked either the ability or the will to make decisions and
that he did not understand the workings of the University
budget. When someone asked him what he had against
Frank, he replied, "Nothing except that he does not get
there." In December, 1930, when governor-elect La Follette
sat in on Frank's presentation of the University's budget requests, he heard Kronshage point out all sorts of minor errors and reproach Frank for balking on the "dead wood" issue. The Regent grumbled openly: "I notice that a lot of
faculty members who we all agreed in 1925 had reached the
limit of their usefulness and should be tied to the post, have
been given material salary increases."[24] La Follette joined the
assault and from then on he too found fault with most aspects of Frank's administration.

Certain rumors claimed that La Follette's animosity resulted from a social break between his wife and Mrs. Glenn
Frank. If such a break occurred, it had no bearing on the
situation. The important factor was that in the course of
the 1930 budget hearings La Follette—already the holder of
grave reservations about Frank's performance—concluded
once and for all that he was an inadequate president. Nor
was the governor mollified when Frank later heaped praise
upon him at a state banquet. "Massachusetts breeds an
Adams family and, through several lifetimes, the Adams'
genius, consecrated to public service, brings its offerings to
state and nation," declared Frank. "Tonight we are bringing the tribute of our own gratitude to the latest and finest
flowering of the like tradition of consecrated genius. . . .
To Governor La Follette, mothered by a shy greatness and
fathered by a fighting genius, to the First Citizen and to
the First Lady of Wisconsin, I ask you to drink with me a
toast."[25]

Beginning in 1931, the break with La Follette, the situation inside the University, and the financial emergency caused by the Depression blighted Frank's relations with a majority of the members of the legislature. Frank especially antagonized legislators by submitting budget requests which exceeded the amount of funds available. Progressives then grew noticeably cool to his handling of University affairs. Some Republicans and Democrats joined in questioning his competence, either out of conviction or because they enjoyed embarrassing a man appointed by a Progressive Board of Regents. Assemblymen and senators alike did more than cut the budgets that Frank submitted. They went out of their way to clash with him at meetings of the joint finance committee and to make derogatory remarks about him in floor debates. They hinted that he allowed oleomargarine in the Memorial Union, claimed that he spent too much time outside the state, asserted that he encouraged a disproportionate number of out-of-state students to attend the University, and denounced the size of his salary. "It's a crime," grumbled one assemblyman, "for a man to receive that much money while there are many people in the state on the verge of starvation and without the normal necessities of life." To embarrass Frank his opponents introduced bills providing for his removal as an *ex officio* member of the Board of Regents and placing a $6,000 limit on the annual salaries of state employees. Although these measures failed to pass, they were symptomatic of the rising dissatisfaction with the University's president. And more and more, Frank found that legislators reacted coldly as he lobbied in the local hotels.[26]

Without much success Frank defended his budgets, offered to co-operate with the legislature in combating the Depression, and boasted that he had made the University one of the best in the nation. He shrugged off complaints about his salary with the explanation that he spent more money performing his duties than he received. Furthermore, he claimed that his frequent trips to other states benefited the University. Instead of resorting to costly trips financed out of public funds to maintain contacts helpful to the University, he explained, he often accepted private speaking invitations.$^{\pi}$ The inference was that, while Frank derived financial benefits from his travels, the University was the real beneficiary. Frank's lectures supposedly redounded to the credit of the University and the state. Plausible though this rationale appeared to Glenn Frank, his critics remained unconvinced by his attempts to justify his behavior.

As Frank became more controversial, malicious rumors circulated concerning his conduct and standard of living. It was said that he boasted in private that he intended to use the University presidency as a steppingstone to the presidency of the United States. It was said that he refused to speak to students when he walked from his car to his office. It was said that he had so many enemies that he had trouble finding people to eat lunch with. It was said that when he attended football games he demanded a place inside the stadium for his automobile. It was said that a famous University leader thought so little of him that he insulted him before several important Wisconsin political leaders. These and similar stories were sometimes even repeated by normally responsible, reliable people. Eventually it became impossible to separate fact from fiction.

Frank's wife, especially, became the butt of gossip, particularly about the social functions held at the presidential mansion even after other state administrators, including the governor, stopped entertaining for reasons of austerity. Mrs. Frank, it was said, exploited students by using them as servants, brought in butlers from Chicago for special occasions, imported black caviar for her guests, spoke repeatedly about becoming the First Lady of the land, refused to speak to faculty wives whose husbands were not full professors or deans, and generally exhibited vulgar social aspirations. Some rumors even claimed that Mrs. Frank's extravagance caused her husband to put his own financial interests above those of the University.

Ernest Meyer, a *Capital Times* reporter renowned in

President Frank at work in his office in Bascom Hall.

The President's sleek limousine—and a student lam-poon of it in a University parade in 1926.

PREXY'S PRIVATE PACKARD

4

Alexander Meiklejohn.

Glenn Frank addressing the class of 1927 at commencement.

Frank entertaining Charles Lindbergh (seated at left) at a football game; and supervising the groundbreaking for the University's Memorial Union, 1925.

The Sportsman's Creed

I stood in the steaming quarters of a football team and listened to the coach talk to the players between the halves of a hard-fought game.

Into a few minutes of flaming speech the coach crowded the whole philosophy of healthy-minded sportsmanship, and I went back to my seat in the stadium with the impression of a creed of sportsmanship, as definite and as dominating as the creeds of religion drafted by the church fathers.

The sportsman would probably cast his creed in the form of a series of determinations rather than a series of dogmas, somewhat as follows:

1. I will not break training, for the satisfactions of achievment are more durable than the satisfactions of appetite.

2. I will not give up in the midst of a contest just because I may be, at the moment, tired or discouraged, for, save in rare instances of utter exhaustion, there are always untapped levels of energy upon which men may call, and I am in honor bound to my fellow players to give to the contest the untapped levels as well as the surface layer of my energy.

3. I will subordinate my playing to the playing of the team, for I have no right to let my vanity stand in the way of victory, to sacrifice sportsmanship for the spotlight, or to trade group achievement for personal applause.

4. I will keep my head however hard I am hit, for to lose my temper is treason to the team, since I cannot have a cool head and a hot temper at the same time.

5. I will be modest in victory, knowing that if I have kept the faith of the sportsman in play, the victory is but the common product of the combined play of my fellows, even if I gave a star performance at a critical moment, and knowing that the moment of victory is life's severest test of a man's character.

6. I will be game in defeat, for only the weakling whines when the fortunes of contest run against him.

Here, I submit, is a magnificent charter of character and conduct.

It was a sense of this creed of sportsmanship, I suppose, that led some one to say long ago that the battle of Waterloo was won on the playing fields of Eton, for these principles of conduct are fundamental alike to the good soldier and to the great statesman.

I am not suggesting that the boy who practices these principles on the football field will automatically practice them in politics or in business; unhappily there seems not to be any such automatic transfer. I am suggesting rather that he must practice and perfect such conduct in all fields as well as on the football field.

GLENN FRANK.

A sample of Frank's philosophy which appeared in a Wisconsin football program in 1927.

George Clarke Sellery.

Governor Philip F. La Follette.

Michael B. Olbrich.

Theodore Kronshage.

Glenn Frank in academic garb.

Madison for his caustic humor, drew upon the rumors for a vitriolic article in the *American Mercury* of January, 1934, entitled "Journalist on Parole." Undoubtedly, he wrote with the approval of highly placed Progressive leaders. Meyer called Frank an "aging boy wonder" and depicted him as a "Pollyanna piping in a daisy patch." He lambasted all aspects of his administration and ridiculed his personality. "He still retains a shining school-boy face and the enduring adolescence of a confirmed optimist. He is, in looks, gestures, diction, and elocution, disarmingly smooth. He smokes a democratic pipe. He laughs easily, but is quite humorless. He makes you feel instantly at ease with him, relaxed, even if you came with a grudge and complaint. He laves your hurts with the balm of his voice, mellow and musical, and weaves around you the spell of his dialectic. He knows words, good, wholesome words, trigger words that release mystical springs in you and make you itch with undefinable enterprise. But when you leave him, it takes less than an hour's walk in the crisp air to recall that your complaint was unanswered, your demands unfilled, and that once again your weapons have remained ingloriously stuck in the syrup of his eloquence. . . . It took the campus two years to doubt him, and six to regard him with amused contempt. And today, eight years after his arrival, he has probably not a single sincere admirer left among the host who hailed his coming with hosannas."[28]

Frank received advanced word of the publication of Meyer's article. In a long letter reviewing and justifying his administration, Frank urged Zona Gale to submit a rebuttal article. He accurately predicted how Meyer intended to "debunk" him, but professed not to understand why Meyer and others considered him a "bogus liberal." Frank noted that he "stood consistently and firmly for that freedom of faculty and student opinion which is an important aspect of university liberalism," that his appointees showed "a constant role of liberal minds," and that he had cleaned the University's wartime record of illiberalism by reinstating credits denied to Meyer who in 1918 had been penalized for being a conscientious objector. Frank thought that the best example of the basic liberalism of his administration was "the large number of persons on the faculty and among the students who are dissatisfied with our system and feel free to say so."[29]

Zona Gale's rebuttal article appeared in a spring issue of the *American Mercury*.[30] It was not the only support Frank received. Numerous others rallied to his defense. Several faculty members wrote letters to the newspapers, denouncing Meyer's methods. A faculty committee, a majority of whose membership was critical of Frank, nevertheless expressed regret over "the undignified and unsportsmanlike attack." Even the controversial architect, Frank Lloyd Wright, one of Wisconsin's most famous citizens, issued a statement protesting the criticism of Frank. He blamed Frank's troubles on a system in which the university president was "a hired man and has to satisfy those who hired him and keep him on the job."[31] For a few brief weeks and months Frank's stock rose once more. But the instinctive reaction of many people to rally to his defense gradually gave way to the old dissatisfactions with the way that he was administering the University. Soon only memories of the article remained—along with new rumors and new doubts.

To a degree Frank's problems could be attributed to the Great Depression and the brutal impact it had on all phases of American life. But this was only part of the story. Many of the campus conflicts would never have occurred had Frank been a more astute administrator and had he kept his fingers closer to the pulse of the University community. Frank's basic difficulty was that, for all his fine words, he proved unable to translate his ideas into reality. He never understood that people interested in the University expected him to do more than formulate ideas, establish committees, make appointments, defend academic freedom, and lobby for increased appropriations. He never understood that his failure to deal with problems which at the moment did not seem pressing could eventually impair his effectiveness, nor that many of his critics on the faculty had a genuine love for the traditions of the University and that they did not oppose him simply for reasons of jealousy or because they enjoyed a good fight. He never understood the emotional attachment that the La Follette family and many leading Progressives had for the University of Wisconsin. He never understood that, because nothing had been said about his failure to honor his pledge to give up his newspaper column, the Board of Regents resented his extracurricular employment. He never understood that the public resented his high standard of living, his decision to send his boy to an expensive Eastern prep school, and his failure to adjust his scale of entertaining to the circumstances prevailing during the Great Depression.

What he understood least of all was how to grow in the job. That he enjoyed a high measure of success for as long as he did was largely because of his ability to project a favorable public image. Throughout, Frank retained his reputation for being charming company, for he remained a gifted lecturer who was always able to sway crowds with his resonant rhetoric. Though some of his shortcomings were apparent to a few people from the start, the public at large did not see them until the Depression and the campus controversies of the 1930's magnified them a thousandfold.

By the close of 1935 Frank's position was rapidly deteriorating. Criticism was mounting against his administration. The bitterness engendered by the salary waivers clearly ran deep within the faculty. The "Rocking Chair" affair and the later controversies in the Extension Division and the department of athletics brought complaints that Frank had not only moved too slowly in making administrative changes, but that when under pressure he had vacillated. He had defended academic freedom, but this was no more than the University had a right to expect of him. But the charges of communist infiltration in the University and the criticism made by Meyer, however unfounded, served to damage his reputation among the uninformed, and no matter how assiduously Frank cultivated support through speaking engagements he was unable to regain public esteem.

Of all his troubles, the break with Philip La Follette loomed the most serious. Frank could survive the animosity of such men as Dean Sellery and of a large number of faculty members. He could withstand charges that he was an ineffective administrator if only because few citizens knew how a good one was expected to perform or how a university operated. He could also withstand attacks by such politicians as Chapple and Burnette. He could not, however, long withstand La Follette's opposition—providing La Follette continued to control the state government—for among the governor's executive responsibilities was that of naming the Board of Regents, and from 1931 onward he appointed men who believed that Frank was a poor administrator.

IX

"Frank Must Go"

EVENTS MOVED SLOWLY and then swiftly towards the
the removal of Glenn Frank as president of the University
of Wisconsin. Three considerations kept him from being
removed before 1937: the political situation in Wisconsin,
the Great Depression, and the composition of the Board of
Regents. Until 1936, Philip Fox La Follette was a minority
governor. In 1934, he had won the governorship for the second time and over two other candidates, but his margin of
victory was small and his Progressive party lacked a majority
in the legislature. Since La Follette's opponents charged that
he wanted personal power, the governor feared the political
repercussions of any overt attempt to remove Frank. Besides,
the Depression had virtually bankrupted the State of Wisconsin. The problems of raising money to run the government
and to carry on Wisconsin's "little New Deal" required most
of the governor's time and energy. "We formed the best
judgment we could," La Follette said, "often in difficult circumstances in the depression years, and then went ahead and
acted rather than do nothing."[1] Finally, there was the Board
of Regents. Because members served staggered six-year terms,
it was not until 1936 that a majority of the fifteen Regents
owed their appointments to Philip La Follette.

Early in 1936, the governor reportedly discussed Frank's
presidency with a group of reporters from Wisconsin newspapers in an off-the-record press conference. All present

supposedly advised him to remove Frank, but if indeed there was such a conference it produced no immediate action. Despite his dissatisfaction with affairs inside the University, La Follette had more pressing problems to worry about. Moreover, he had no direct jurisdiction in the matter. He had made his position clear on December 16, 1935, when he had told a reporter from the *Wisconsin State Journal,* "My only power in the conduct of the University is the appointment of regents to administer the institution."

However, La Follette reluctantly became involved in the chain of circumstances which led to Frank's removal. In February, 1936, Harold Wilkie, the president of the Board of Regents, called on La Follette. Wilkie, a 1912 graduate of the University of Wisconsin Law School, had been appointed by La Follette. He claimed that he had told the governor that a majority of the Regents had lost confidence in Frank. A few days later Wilkie saw the governor again. He brought with him two Regents, Daniel Grady and John Callahan, both of whom had been members of the Board which eleven years earlier had selected Frank as president. There is some confusion over what transpired. Wilkie said that both Grady and Callahan repeatedly told La Follette that the handling of the Snell case several months before had convinced them that Frank was incompetent. The governor and the three Regents then agreed that Frank should be asked to resign, effective June 30, 1936, and that Callahan would discuss the matter with Frank. Wilkie also went to see Frank, who in turn visited Wilkie's law office. Evidently, Frank agreed to leave quietly. He acknowledged that an open hearing would impair his career and he requested time to find a new position. But the Board of Regents failed to ask Frank for a letter of resignation, a mistake it later regretted.[2]

Actually, Frank had no intention of leaving without a fight. Shortly after these conversations he began to campaign against what he called "Governor La Follette's plan to run the University for political purposes." Frank rallied to his standard newspaper editors whose friendship he had sought over the years, alumni leaders who had found him witty and entertaining, old friends such as Zona Gale, and business-men who deplored "La Follettism."[3]

Although La Follette and some of the Regents had agreed among themselves to remove Frank, they failed to take the initiative and were soon caught in an embarrassing impasse. Early in March, 1936, several newspapers reported that Progressive members of the Board of Regents intended to press for Frank's resignation and on March 11, before the start of a regularly scheduled meeting of the Board, Wilkie admitted to reporters that he and La Follette had discussed Frank's leaving the University.[4] A more inept method of handling a critical piece of University business would be hard to imagine. But if Wilkie was caught off guard, the same could not be said for Frank, who now categorically denied that he had resigned.

After an embarrassing silence, the routine meeting began. Nothing further was said about Frank's tenure at the University. There would be no immediate showdown. Although a majority of the Regents may have lost confidence in Frank, they were not willing to carry their evaluation to its logical conclusion. Perhaps they believed that Frank was too powerful to be removed without a struggle; perhaps they preferred to await the outcome of the fall election.

Throughout the middle months of 1936, Frank and his opponents sparred back and forth. Frank tried to depict himself as the intended victim of a Progressive attempt to control the University. He asserted that "political domination . . . produces a reptile University to serve political ends," and persuaded a supporter to compare La Follette's attitude toward the University with that of Huey Long's toward Louisiana State University. "The alumni of the University had better wake up and get this thing before someone offers the State University to the highest bidder," declared a Frank partisan in the *Wisconsin Alumni Magazine*. La Follette did not reply. He was busy campaigning for re-election. His Progressive majority on the Board of Regents, however, sought to embarrass Frank by attacking the preliminary budget which had been formulated for submission to the next legislature. In the course of a stormy six-hour meeting in June, Frank implied that he might resign if Regents made any changes in his financial proposals. A month later, on July 26, and by "sheer force of numbers"—the vote was eight to five—the Board rejected Frank's budget and ordered him to submit a new one prepared by Wilkie. Despite this embarrassing setback, Frank came out of the meeting denying that he intended to resign. "There is no truth whatever to such reports," he announced. Nothing further happened until the election. Then, on November 6, 1936, La Follette swept the state in a landslide victory, and few believed that Frank could last the rest of the academic year.[5]

The machinery designed to bring about Frank's removal began to turn early the next month. On December 9, Wilkie again asked Frank to resign. "Operating behind a screen of the most painstaking secrecy," said a reporter, "progressive regent leadership poised the ax for almost immediate descent when they summoned Frank to a conference this morning, locked the doors and reportedly told him that the time had come to make a graceful exit." Frank refused to commit himself. Next La Follette, Wilkie, and Clough Gates, another Progressive Regent, supposedly held a strategy conference. A few days later a "prominent professor," acting for Wilkie, sounded out Dean George Sellery. Should the Regents press forward with their plan to force Frank's resignation? How would the faculty react in such an eventuality? The dean replied, "For Heaven's sake don't drop the case; don't leave it unsettled, hanging over our heads, for the tension is very disturbing; settle it one way or the other." Sellery also indicated his belief that the majority of faculty members would readily acquiesce in the Board's action. Not long afterwards La Follette called Sellery away from a party to ask if the dean would serve as acting president in the event that Frank should be dismissed. Sellery answered that he would if he were appointed. Obviously the anti-Frank Regents wanted no last-minute complications.[6]

On the morning of December 16, 1936, Frank was present at a regularly scheduled open meeting of the Board of Regents. A large number of students crowded the smoke-befogged committee room in Bascom Hall. There the Regents addressed each other in overly friendly, first-name terms as they struggled to give the appearance of a calm, congenial meeting. But all present—the Regents, President Frank, the students—sensed the underlying tension; all realized that the University was at a major turning point. Then, without fanfare, Wilkie read a list of charges against Frank. He asserted that Frank had mishandled the University's finances, lost the confidence of the Board and faculty, failed to lead, spent too much time away from the campus, used public money for his own benefit, and improperly managed the institution's affairs. "Frank must go," he concluded.

By the time that Wilkie had read his list of charges the room was in a confused uproar. Some students shouted "Down with Wilkie!" Others pressed for Frank's resignation. Then the Regents fell to arguing among themselves, with Wilkie and Grady—now Frank's strongest supporter on the Regents, much to the surprise of the press and the consternation of the La Follette forces—hotly disputing the issue.[7] When Frank finally got an opportunity to be heard he declared emphatically that he would not resign. Despite the seeming determination of the majority of the Board to rid the University of Frank, the meeting took no formal action. Thus an impasse had once more been reached with the Regents asking for and Frank refusing to give his resignation.[8]

The irony of this situation was underscored less than forty-eight hours later when Frank appeared before La Follette to read a budget statement prepared by Wilkie. Except for some forced smiles, a feeling of expectancy in the audience, and some ironic asides, there was little hint of trouble.[9] It was a deceptive calm. Actually, the battle lines were already and openly drawn.

Shortly before Christmas the Board of Regents ordered Frank to show cause in a public hearing why he should be retained. Frank objected to the date, January 7, 1937, con-

tending that he needed at least four weeks to prepare a statement. The Regents ignored his plea. The call for the hearing caused comment throughout Wisconsin. Zona Gale
pledged her support to Frank. She accused La Follette of
desecrating his father's memory and urged the public to telegraph the Board of Regents asking that Frank be retained.
Newspaper opinion generally divided along partisan lines,
with the anti-La Follette papers charging that the removal
proceedings were politically inspired. However, the usually
anti-La Follette *Milwaukee Journal* supported Frank's retirement "because," it said, "he has not been a successful University head." Significantly, Frank's following was not as
vocal as it had been earlier. Neither Zona Gale nor the newspapers succeeded in arousing public opinion on Frank's behalf, and many of his supporters remained silent. No deluge
of telegrams swamped the Regents; even the alumni association—whose officers reportedly approved of Frank—declined
to aid him; the faculty was almost ominously quiet. John
Chapple, who had branded both Frank and La Follette as
promoters of communist ideas, probably reflected the attitude of many of La Follette's opponents when he declared,
"It doesn't mean anything particular to us for we're 'agin'
em both, but the procedure seems a bit strange."[10]

The hearing began as scheduled on the morning of January 6, 1937, in the same committee room on the first floor
of Bascom Hall where years before another Board of Regents
had voted to offer Frank the presidency of the University.[11]
Adding to the drama was the presence of three members of
the older Board: Grady and Callahan as Regents, and Zona
Gale as an interested spectator. The small room overflowed
with Regents, newspapermen, students, and alumni. Everyone seemed uncomfortable. Flash bulbs popped almost constantly. Perspiration poured from photographers' faces as
they leaned over the backs of the Regents to obtain better
angles for their pictures. Reporters who had to get messages
off to their offices in Milwaukee, Chicago, or New York had
to force their way out of the room, with little hope of re-

gaining admittance. On the outside of the building students crowded at the windows to obtain a view of the proceedings. Inside, a swaying and milling mob blocked the halls, despite the efforts of fire department officials. There were many rooms on the campus larger than the committee room, but the Regents rejected all requests that they move. Ignoring the fact that a larger room would have permitted more orderly proceedings, they explained that they did not want to give the impression that they were conducting a "Star Chamber" investigation. In the circumstances, the explanation was as weak as it was unconvincing.

The crux of the proceedings consisted of lengthy statements by Wilkie, Gates, and Frank. Wilkie surveyed most of the major charges which had been made over the years against Frank. Gates went over the same ground but elaborated on some points. Wilkie, a trial lawyer, was at his best. He declared that two basic reasons necessitated Frank's removal —his "lack of essential qualifications for the position" which in turn created "a lack of confidence in him on the part of those with whom he must deal," and his "unsatisfactory" arrangement "as regards salary and other emoluments." Wilkie then unleashed a flurry of accusations. Frank had failed to prepare the budget on time. "Every year since I have been on the board," Wilkie asserted, "his attention has been called to this, but his many engagements have never permitted him to get the budget to us in season." Frank had also prepared the budget in a careless manner. "In some instances," Wilkie reported, "criticism by the business office had not been secured at all before the budgets have been submitted to the regents." Too, Frank had lacked the courage to formulate an equitable salary-waiver system. In Wilkie's view, "He was a reluctant follower, never a leader." In addition, he was a weak executive lacking "the courage and capacity" to formulate plans, make recommendations, and frame methods for carrying them out. According to Wilkie, Frank had mishandled the Extension and athletic controversies by taking equivocal positions. Frank had also lived too lavishly, and at the expense of the University. There were other charges as well: Frank had used his position to acquire an unfounded reputation as an educator; he had provided "window dressing instead of real education and executive service"; he had lost the confidence of the people; and he had not "been wise enough to resign." While Wilkie spoke, Frank kept saying, "That is manifestly false, Mr. Wilkie," or "That isn't true."

Frank briefly opened his defense late in the day, then resumed after an overnight adjournment. Grimly, he reviewed his administration and refuted his accusers, blaming most of his problems on the times. "Mr. Wilkie conveniently ignores the fact that for seven of the eleven years I have been chief executive of the University, the nation has been passing through the most drastic depression in its history," he declared. Under the circumstances, Frank felt that he had done an excellent job of making administrative decisions, solving internal problems, and providing the Regents with clear budget information. He repeated his claim that the duties of his office required him to spend more money than he received in salary, and he scoffed at the assertion that he spent too much time away from the University. "Institutions," he asserted, "do not forge forward—as this University has forged forward—by accident or with the millstone of an inattentive administration around their neck." Admitting that he did not know every item of the budget, he nevertheless contended that "The president of no university in America has such knowledge." With a feeling of pride he described the budgetary procedures which he had instituted to provide the University with a clear analysis of its needs, and challenged "Wilkie to prove, if he can, that the University of Wisconsin does not have . . . as complete, competent, and business-like procedures in the preparation and presentation of budgets as any industry on the American continent."[12] Frank concluded that there was no evidence that the people of Wisconsin had lost confidence in his administration. "Since this assertion by Mr. Wilkie has been given wide publicity, I have been receiving by telephone, by telegraph, by letter, and by personal calls expressions of unqualified confidence from every nook and corner of the State and the Nation, from members of the faculty, from former regents, from former and present members of the legislature regardless of party, from officials of the State, from farmers, from workers in industry, from merchants, from the operators of filling stations, from lawyers, from doctors, from mothers of students, from alumni, from men and women in all walks of life."

As soon as Frank completed his defense, his supporters carried out what the newspaper men called a last stand. Regent Grady, an impressive, silver-haired figure, eloquently defended Frank with the argument that fifty years before the enemies of Robert La Follette, Sr., had dismissed President John Bascom in the same room, thus blackening the reputation of the University. Now, declared Grady, a son of Old Bob had deserted the principles of his illustrious father by commissioning Wilkie to act as a "judge, jury, and prosecutor." Pointing at Wilkie, he asserted, "While you have the power of votes, you have not the right to go ahead with this thing." Some students responded with cheers and a "skyrocket" yell, but an anti-Frank Regent snapped, "We've been stalling long enough. We should get down to business and get it over with." At that moment Zona Gale bobbed up dramatically from the sweltering mass. Most knew that she had terminated her friendship with Governor La Follette to defend Frank. As flash bulbs bathed her in flickering light she spoke movingly, condemning the hearing as a trial, applauding Frank's liberalism, and arguing that his influence on students had always been beneficent. After Zona Gale disappeared back into the crowd other speakers clamored to be heard. An alumnus talked of "star chambering," a graduate student implored the thoroughly exasperated Regents to remember the "Wisconsin Spirit," and a state senator characterized Frank as a "friend of the farmers." Individual Regents badgered the speakers and engaged in unseemly wrangling among themselves. The air of tension seldom eased, except when Wilkie acknowledged Frank with a crisp, "Mr. President," and Frank drew a laugh with his response—"For the time being." Finally, the Regents tired of the round of repetitious speeches and recessed for supper. The crowd hooted and hollered.

A few hours later the evening session began in an atmosphere crackling with tension. A huge crowd milled around outside the committee room, students smashed the windows in an effort to hear, and a woman fainted. Others chanted, "One, two, three, four, open the door," while "huskies" and police fought to stop their advance. Outwardly cheerful, Frank and Wilkie sat side by side as the president's supporters, striving to overcome "unbridled confusion," read hurriedly prepared statements. But a Regent complained, "I'm tired of all this stuff. Let's finish it now." Wilkie then denied Frank permission to read a statement and without further ado the Board of Regents voted on the question of removing Frank from the presidency of the University. The crowd listened in hushed silence as Secretary of the Board Richard McCaffrey called the roll alphabetically. Thus Wilkie voted last, and with obvious satisfaction cast the deciding ballot against Frank. For the record, McCaffrey intoned "Eight regents voted aye and seven no."[13] Frank had ceased to be president of the University of Wisconsin. He slammed shut his brief case with the comment, "I consider it a distinct compliment to be voted against by a board like this," then stalked away to his automobile. It carried him down the hill from Bascom Hall and away from the campus of the University of Wisconsin.

The next day Frank held a press conference at which he declared, "I went through this public hearing only because certain principles of the University were at stake. . . . If the alert press can't recognize a political firing squad when it sees one, I'm not going to discuss it." As he spoke, Dean Sellery moved into the president's office. Outside, some students threw snowballs at the windows. Another, larger group of students cut classes, marched to the State Capitol and disrupted a La Follette press conference at which the governor blamed Frank for interjecting politics into University affairs, repeated many of the charges made at the hearing, and explained his role in the removal. "It was not the responsibility of the governor to decide what he might do were he a regent," La Follette stated. "It was only his duty to be satisfied that there were substantial grounds upon which regents, acting in the best interests of the University, could conclude that it would benefit the University to change administrations." After disrupting the conference the students moved on to the assembly chamber and demanded that La Follette appear before them. In a few minutes La Follette shouldered his way through the crowd and mounted the rostrum. He made a short extemporaneous speech. He spoke of his father's contributions to the University and closed with a statement about the greatness of the University of Wisconsin. Then, while most of the students cheered, he left the chamber. With that the protest demonstration ended. The students quietly filed out. A few agitators called for a march to Frank's home to demonstrate their loyalty, but no one paid any attention—it was too close to the lunch hour.[14]

Wisconsin newspapers devoted a great deal of space to Frank's dismissal. Editorially, they divided along partisan political lines. The reactions of the two Madison newspapers were fairly typical. William Evjue, publisher of the pro-La Follette *Capital Times,* lauded the Regents' decision. "Glenn Frank has fallen because he yielded to the temptation inspired by a vaulting personal ambition. As a result he subordinated the welfare of the University to self-interest. . . . As the years went on it soon became evident that Frank more and more began to have one eye trained on the White House. Indeed, the president's wife was frequently quoted as saying that her husband would some day sit in the White House. This inner ambition of Glenn Frank soon began to be reflected in the administration of the University. Every major problem that came to President Frank's desk was considered from the angle, of the effect it would have on Mr. Frank's political ambitions." On the other hand the editor of the anti-La Follette *Wisconsin State Journal* took an opposite tack, contending that La Follette sought personal power and that he had removed Frank in order to dominate the University.[15]

Frank received many expressions of support from businessmen. One manufacturer telegraphed, "Congratulate you heartily first on your separation from University of Wisconsin and second for the manner in which separation was accomplished." The head of the Wisconsin Alumni Association apologized for being unable to rally the organization behind Frank during the proceedings but declared, "your reputation and prestige have been increased by the events of the last thirty days." In Boston, Edward Filene, Frank's old employer, announced that he continued to hold Frank in his highest esteem, while the wife of a Milwaukee industrialist wondered, "How can people be so low and hateful!"[16]

Some faculty members also supported Frank. But, as Sellery had predicted, the faculty was generally content to play a watching role, and when the time came for the faculty to take a formal stand it merely acknowledged the Regents' authority to deal with such strictly administrative matters. Coming as it did from a faculty so jealous of its prerogatives, especially in advising on matters of general policy and academic freedom, this resolution underscored the unwillingness of the faculty to give Frank its positive support. Indeed, there was also general relief that Frank was no longer president.[17]

Acting-President Sellery, in a speech before the faculty on January 11, 1937, quickly set the tone for his interim administration. "It is neither my duty nor my desire to pass judgment on the rights and wrongs of the recent upheaval. I wish merely to make a brief profession of faith. . . . It is sometimes forgotten that regents, presidents and deans, and all of the other administrative officials of a University exist for the sole purpose of enabling the teaching and research staffs to do their jobs. The administrators are in the strictest sense helpers. It is bad for the administrators to get into a snarl; but at the worst the teaching and research staffs can still carry on for a time in spite of such a snarl. And this you have done to your eternal credit. . . . And now for my profession of faith. And in listening to it I beg you not to think that I am making comparisions, directly or indirectly. I explicitly disclaim them. First, I am a faculty man, bred in the faculty points of view and convinced of the superior wisdom of faculty conclusions in the matters entrusted to the faculty by the laws of the University. I shall regard it as my duty during the few months of my tenure to represent the faculty decisions and desires in matters confided to the faculty before the Board of Regents. Secondly, I believe in faculty tenure, not so much for the protection of those who are now on the faculty as for the guarantee it affords that we shall be able to attract to our faculty young men of promise and capacity. Thirdly, I believe in straightening out certain salary inequalities as fast as our means permit. Finally, I believe in the greatness and worth of the University of Wisconsin and of the State of Wisconsin, which created and nurtures it. We are still a great University and we shall continue to advance in greatness and worth with the State. We are both, State and University, sound in heart and head. Do not, I beg of you, sell the University or the State of Wisconsin short! *Sursum corda!* (Lift up your hearts!) "[18] Thus, Sellery closed the door on what he would one day call "The Glenn Frank Regime."

X

Greener Pastures

THE NEWSPAPERS CALLED THE REMOVAL of Glenn Frank from the presidency of the University of Wisconsin the first defeat of his career. If it was a defeat, it was a calculated one. Given the choice of resigning quietly (perhaps coupled with an announcement that he was to take up another, even more responsible post), or forcing the Board of Regents to dismiss him, Frank had deliberately chosen the latter course. Perhaps he believed that the Board would retract rather than have its decision exposed to a public hearing; perhaps he thought that he would be exonerated; or perhaps he thought that the people of Wisconsin would rally to his support and force the Board to rescind its decision. Yet Frank must have known that the tide of opinion in the Regents, the University, the legislature, and the state as a whole was running against him. This had been demonstrated as early as July 26, 1936, when the Regents humiliated him with their rejection of his budget recommendations, and again in November when Governor La Follette won a sweeping victory at the polls. And Frank must have realized that a public hearing would put him on the defensive by obliging him to show cause why he should not be dismissed.

Frank's insistence upon a removal hearing stemmed from his political ambitions. Whether a majority of Regents succeeded in forcing him out of office or not, Frank believed that he, not they, would emerge victorious. The turmoil of a public hearing could be expected to strengthen the anti-La

Follette forces in the state and to make Frank the rallying point for such opposition. As a man harboring ambitions to be President of the United States, it was essential, of course, that Frank emerge from the hearing not as an unsuccessful educational administrator but as a martyr to the cause of academic freedom, as a courageous man whose career and reputation had been trampled upon by a power-hungry governor.

For years, Frank had carefully nurtured his political aspirations. Although he had avoided formally identifying himself with either major party, since gravitating from New York his sympathies were with the Republicans. Most of his friends were Republican businessmen who approved of his approach to the issues of the day and particularly to his favorite contention that the problems of the machine age could best be solved by "industrial statesmen." Moreover, he was on good terms with two Republican Presidents. He vacationed in northern Wisconsin during the summer of 1928 with Calvin Coolidge, and he visited Herbert Hoover at the White House. These associations, especially with President Hoover, fed Frank's ambitions.

Frank considered that Hoover had the ability and the opportunity to be a great President. On May 4, 1929, six months before the onslaught of the Depression, Frank wrote Hoover, "I believe that the next few years will afford an unusual opportunity for the leadership of opinion throughout Western Civilization on the human potentialities of the social order that is being produced by science and technology. The social implications of this new order seem to me to underline the realistic politics which, I know, is your fundamental concern. There are dawning insights about us, but they have not yet been coordinated and made articulate. On the one hand are scholar-publicists who do not quite see the deepest tendencies and possibilities. On the other hand are great businessmen who see fragments of the picture. . . . A great historic opportunity is yours to interpret to Western Civilization the human possibilities locked up in its scientifico-technological economy, an economy which if left uninterpreted affords regrettable targets for demagogic attacks." After the collapse of the economy, Frank told Hoover that he found it "refreshing to know that the nation is under the leadership of a man with both background and foresight and a keen sense of contemporary trends."[1]

During the 1930's Frank became the darling of an articulate and influential segment of the "business wing" of the Republican party. In the process he became a partisan politician. His daily newspaper column commented less and less upon the "good life" and more and more upon the economic ramifications of the New Deal. Two books compiled from his "editorials," *Thunder and Dawn* (1932) and *America's Hour of Decision* (1934), appealed to businessmen, and Frank increasingly geared his speeches to them. Economic conservatives, in particular, found his ideas attractive. Among the thousands of letters he received was one from Robert R. McCormick, the publisher of the Republican *Chicago Tribune,* who wrote in 1934, "Your speech on economic conditions, which I was fortunate enough to read in this morning's paper, is outstandingly the best that has been presented in these troublesome times." After Frank spoke in Chicago at a "Century of Progress" dinner the same year, 1934, Alfred Sloan, Jr., president of the General Motors Corporation and a major contributor to the Republican party, told him, "It was undoubtedly the most outstanding talk of the evening. It was direct; very much to the point, and struck, as I am sure you appreciate, a sympathetic chord among every individual present, to which I should add, those of the radio audience." Theodore Roosevelt, Jr., whose economic views differed from those held by his father, also praised Frank. "I am sure you are hitting the right note. Our people are fussed and dissatisfied with the folly and self-seeking of the present administration. . . . When you are next in New York won't you let me know and lunch or dine with me."[2]

These were the comments that Frank liked to hear. They, too, nurtured his political aspirations.

Throughout the Depression, Frank considered himself a "liberal," and he sometimes complained about the way his admirers failed to grasp the meaning of his message. In 1934, he remarked with sincere exasperation on the interpretation placed on a speech he had given in Chicago. "One editor after another made me out a blind ass, patting the business man on the back, absolving him from all blame for the spreading paralysis of enterprise, and asserting that nothing is necessary beyond setting the business man free to produce without let or hindrance. . . . I was discouraged rather than delighted because the wildness of applause made me wonder whether many of the men had not wholly overlooked my insistence that there is nothing to do but call a halt on science and technology and go in for a deliberate scaling down of enterprise and living standards unless we deliberately bring our economic policies abreast of our technological process."[3] In a sense, Frank was correct. He never advocated "rugged individualism," the shibboleth of conservative Republicans. However, he did change his views about the Depression and eventually he came to oppose the New Deal of Franklin Delano Roosevelt.

When the Depression started, Frank—in keeping with his previous conclusions—contended that the collapse was a result of the failure of Americans to cope with the problems of the machine age. He enunciated his position with confidence. "Whether we like it or not," he wrote in 1930, "the Old Individualism has rapidly become a matter of record and reminiscence and a corporate America with the possibility of a New Feudalism is being born." The only answer was to give the masses more purchasing power by providing them with a greater share of the wealth. "I know it sounds paradoxical," he said, "but it is to the best interests of business that a larger share of the national income shall find its way into the hands of the masses who buy consumable commodities. . . . The wise captains of industry, in order to make a profit, will more and more have to provide the very things labor and liberalism have through generations pleaded for on the grounds of injustice."[4]

Frank believed that the faltering economy was the fault of men rather than the system; that it came when "an era of over-confidence gave way to an era of over-caution." He was convinced that, if given the right leadership, America would eventually recover and become stronger than ever. In 1932 he stated his basic thesis in the conclusion of his book, *Thunder and Dawn*. "There is genius enough in America to evolve and to execute political and economic policies that will give us, in point of material well-being and enrichment, a future that will far outstrip our feverishly and fleetingly prosperous past. If America does not realize this finer and more fruitful future, and begin her realization of it with decent promptness, it will be either because at the top we suffer a breakdown of political and industrial leadership or because at the bottom the people, in some moment of leaderless confusion, fanatically follow some false prophet from either the ultra-reactionary or the ultra-radical camp. It will not be because the cards of destiny are stacked against us. They are not. Every card in the deck is in our hands. It is a matter of playing them expertly."[5]

For a while Frank felt that Roosevelt's New Deal would head America down the path "toward a new economics that shall take its cue from today's facts rather than yesterday's text books." Although he admitted that he was somewhat dubious about being "ordered about by bureaucrats" and suspected "the long-time soundness of the policy of restricting production and demand," in May, 1933, he announced, "I am not at all alarmed as some observers seem to be, over the extra-ordinary powers lately lodged in the hands of the president. . . . Quite apart from the present emergency, I think we must move in the direction of making the president, in fact as well as theory, the national leader in policy and action, with Congress more and more a body with the utmost freedom of debate for the criticism and clarification of presidential leadership, but less and less a body able to bring about a political paralysis of creative government." He wholeheartedly endorsed the National Recovery Administration (NRA), which sought to revitalize the American business community. Frank gave numerous radio speeches for the NRA Speaker's Bureau and supported the recovery program in his newspaper column. In the last half of 1933 he even declared that opposition to NRA was "treasonable," that NRA represented a "courageous gamble," that NRA might eventually "make strikes permanently unnecessary," and that NRA's strength was Roosevelt's "insistence that we must spread buying power more widely among the working millions who are industry's customers as well as industry's servants."[6] Frank's enchantment with NRA and the New Deal waned suddenly in the spring of 1934. Either out of conviction or because many of his business friends were rapidly becoming outright enemies of all that Roosevelt stood for, he made a series of speeches condemning the New Deal policies of restricting production. He regarded such controls as a threat to personal liberty and democratic self-government. Perhaps because he had been an ardent supporter of NRA only a few short months before, Frank's about face received considerable national publicity and seemed to strike a responsive chord in some of the New Deal's opponents.

Among the people who were impressed with Frank's views were the owners of the McGraw Hill Publishing Company. In June, 1934, a representative of the company suggested to Frank that he write a book, because, "Some of us here are of the opinion that the time has come for someone in authority to speak effectively to the American people on the eventual results of the policies which have been built around the theory of an economic scarcity." Frank was ready to oblige. "The coast-to-coast response I have had to various aspects of this general approach I have advanced in addresses during the last few months leads me to think it would find a wide reading," he said. "If I can actually *do* it as well as I *feel* it, it might have a material influence in shaping the issues around which the 1936 battle will be fought. . . . If you are in a position to gamble rather handsomely on an advance royalty payment, I could junk my other plans and do this within the next thirty days." In the middle of July, the publishers agreed to give Frank an advance of $2,500. He then proceeded over a six-week period to produce a fifty-thousand-word manuscript, which appeared in the early fall of 1934 under the title of *America's Hour of Decision*.

The book was based on his old newspaper columns and speeches. Throughout, he attacked vices which he claimed were inherent in the New Deal program to restrict production, contending that the mistaken belief that the United States needed to develop a "self-contained nationalism" motivated New Deal policy makers. "I am convinced that the current swing toward self-contained Nationalism is a venture in simple mindedness," he wrote. "If unchecked, it will mean the retreat of the civilized modern to primitive tribalism. It will enforce revolutionary readjustments in the organization, capitalization, and operation of our major enterprises. It will make necessary a sweeping political regimentation of business, industry, and agriculture that is repugnant to the American spirit. It will spell the doom of commercial agriculture on this continent, and drive the American farmer to the status of a peasant, with a standard of living higher, perhaps, than the hard lot of the European peasant, but with the subsistence income that makes the peasant nevertheless. It will mean that a baffled statesmenship . . . is setting out to liquidate the age of plenty and lead mankind back to the age of scarcity."[8] *America's Hour of Decision* received mixed notices. Most reviewers said that Frank offered few solutions to the problems which he posed. Frank did not care about the reviews. He received several thousand dollars in royalties, as well as many favorable letters from important Republican leaders to whom he had sent complimentary copies.

The book, his other writings, and his radio and banquet

speeches helped give Frank a national reputation as an articulate and thoughtful opponent of the New Deal. During
1935 and 1936 he broadened his opposition to the Democratic program. He opposed social security on the grounds that
"the average American would rather have security come in
the day-to-day operation of our economic structure than
through artificial schemes of make-work by the government
or elaborate insurance schemes"; he warned that "political
bureaucracy is quite as likely as big business to bite off more
than it can chew"; he claimed that an Alaskan re-settlement
project represented "fuzzy planning that is doomed to fail
and, in the failing, discredit intelligent reform for a generation to come"; he declared that "Roosevelt wants a kind of
government that the Constitution does not provide"; and he
contended that the New Deal was in the process of creating
"a huge arsenal and armory filled with ammunition and
weapons of power to be captured by some yet-to-arise dictatorial government which will mean the end of all our fathers
fought to establish in the American scheme of government."[9]
In the process of enunciating these criticisms Frank shifted
away from some of the positions that he had previously held,
justifying his actions on the basis that the New Deal had
failed to build the "Great Civilization envisioned at its outset." Besides attacking NRA he reversed his 1933 position
that the Congress should vest greater power in the executive
branch of government. In 1935, after an important piece of
Roosevelt's program—the NRA—had been struck down by
the Supreme Court, Frank declared that the justices were
right in insisting that Congress should not delegate blanket
authority to the executive branch to create, in effect, wholly
new legislation, because it was better to suffer some malad-
justments than to set precedents that might become instru-
ments of tyranny.[10]

In Madison an ever-increasing number of politicians and
businessmen had visited Frank at the presidential mansion.
Some, such as Otto Falk and Walter Harnischfeger, both
Milwaukee industrialists, were kingmakers in the Republican
party in Wisconsin. Others, such as Frank Knox, the pub-

lisher of the *Chicago Daily News,* and Ray L. Wilbur, Hoover's Secretary of the Interior and the president of Stanford University, had national political connections. In 1934 Frank had announced that he was a Republican. A year later he had volunteered to speak without a fee at a Republican fundraising dinner in Michigan honoring Senator Arthur H. Vandenberg. Thus politics had increasingly taken up Frank's time, although he admitted that he believed it impossible for a "man to discharge his responsibility for the executive direction of a state university, dependent upon successive legislatures and widely varying political groups for its support, if he participates personally in party conflict."[11]

From time to time people mentioned Frank as a possible candidate for the 1936 Republican nomination for the presidency. He received pledges of support; Eastern columnists actually called him a serious contender; and some Wisconsin newspapers praised his qualifications. An editorial on the front page of the anti-La Follette *Wisconsin State Journal* declared, "Here, in our midst, we have a candidate who has attracted nationwide attention by his charm and brilliancy, and is recognized as one of the outstanding young men of our generation, yet we have done nothing, and are doing nothing, to capitalize this fact. He has forged to the front by the force of his own genius, without push or pull from anyone, and despite the sniping of our witch-doctors and would-be fascists, instead of with our encouragement and support to which he is entitled."[12] This, and similar praise from other newspapers and individuals, seemed to be the beginning of a concerted drive to get the Republican presidential nomination for Frank.

This possibility was strengthened by a mysterious trip that a New York financier, Frank A. Vanderlip, made in March, 1935, on Frank's behalf. Vanderlip, Frank's close friend since the 1920's, talked with several important people "on the situation." They included certain Indiana business leaders, publisher William Randolph Hearst, and Herbert Hoover.[13] Frank seriously contemplated participating in the

1936 Republican National Convention. Perhaps he wanted to be keynote speaker; perhaps he even hoped to gain the nomination. But nothing came of Vanderlip's discussions and in August, 1935, Frank ordered his name off a "GOP Presidential poll." He announced, "I am not in politics and see no point in having my name included."[14] Still, no matter what role Frank decided to play in 1936, there was no doubt that he was in politics and there were rumors that Governor Philip La Follette, who had national political ambitions of his own, did not approve. In fact, some observers thought that there might have been a connection between Frank's growing political importance and the decision to force him out of the University. They claimed that La Follette had concluded that Madison was not big enough for the two of them and that Frank would have to be removed from office.

After Frank left the University of Wisconsin, he concluded that he needed a "voice" in order to continue to inform the public of his views. And thus he decided to return to journalism. At the same time he sought a sound business opportunity. In June, 1937, he became interested in acquiring *Rural Progress,* a monthly magazine of "Rural and General Interest," published in Chicago and distributed free throughout the midwest to some 2,000,000 farming families. Advertising revenues were supposed to provide enough money to pay editorial, printing, and circulation costs, and to leave a tidy profit besides. Since the magazine's founding in 1934, however, it had operated at a loss. Frank was aware of these financial and other drawbacks, for an advertising firm had appraised the property for him. It had reported: "Against the valuable assets and potentials there are certain liability factors; this paper is comparatively new, in the beginning it aroused among advertising agencies a certain amount of prejudice and rancour as it was rumored, truthfully or not, that the publication would enter into 'deals' with advertising agencies and advertisers. It has a 'controlled' circulation and this seems to have been anathema to the advertising profession. . . . Editorially, and from the layout and mechanical standpoint, the publication will have to be revised and dressed up. . . . Special consideration should be given to editorial appeal and reader interest that will prove attractive to the dairy farmer and stock raiser. . . . *Rural Progress* has among the advertising profession, that is among such members as know it at all well, a reputation for pulling power if the direct mail type copy is used. It is not so highly regarded for straight copy or for institutional copy." The agency suggested that if Frank bought the magazine he should stress that he had become editor, that he should place advertisements in business magazines designed to reach small manufacturers, and that he should hire a new advertising man. The report predicted a net profit of $350,000 to $700,000 per annum if each issue contained from thirty to fifty pages of advertising.[15] Frank was confident that he could run the periodical successfully; he had unlimited faith in the power of his own name.

On June 30, 1937, Frank acquired control of *Rural Progress* by persuading several of his wealthy supporters to purchase over $100,000 worth of stock in the magazine. His backers included Wisconsin industrial leaders active in the Republican party; George Rumely, a nationally known agricultural expert; George Ball, an Indiana glass manufacturer; and Frank Vanderlip, Jr., a New York banker. Frank used little of his own money, although he obtained an option to purchase 103,750 shares of common stock at five dollars a share on or before July 1, 1942. In the meantime, he received a proxy from the founder, Maurice Reynolds, to vote his majority holdings. Reynolds was eager to oblige anyone who could bring $100,000 into the company. Frank assumed the title of editor at a salary of $25,000 a year. He also arranged to edit *Rural Progress* from Madison, where in the spring of 1937 he had purchased a large home. In glowing terms he telegraphed his backers: "Have already made gratifying progress on advertising which promises to put property in the black within a reasonable time.'"[16] His optimism proved premature.

Frank announced his assumption of the editorship with as much fanfare as possible. On July 22, 1937, he sent telegrams to fifteen hundred potential advertisers, to whom he described himself in the most flattering of terms. "We doubt that any man in America is better equipped to develop a truly great journal for rural America," Frank wrote. "Under Frank's direction, *Rural Progress* will grind no personal or political axes. It will deal fearlessly with regional and national problems affecting midwestern farm homes, with enriched editorial content for the entire family and authoritative specialized information for farmers as producers and distributors.'"[17]

A statement published in the September, 1937, edition of the magazine called Frank "a great student of Agriculture, a great Scholar, a great Interpreter, a great Editor and above all else, a great American." The statement also claimed, "Circumstances have conspired to make DR. FRANK the best equipped man who ever sat down to a job like this. Though not himself a farmer, he knows agriculture as few men know it . . . he knows its research men who are hammering away at both the science and economics of farming . . . he knows its active leaders in the great farm organizations . . . he knows farmers . . . he has *lived* the problem he is now to deal with in RURAL PROGRESS.'"[18] Frank wrote the statement over the former publisher's name.

In the first issue published under his editorship, Frank set forth lofty goals. He pledged that he would "ransack" the laboratories of all important colleges of agriculture in the country to find the latest methods of raising the quality, increasing the production, and lowering the costs of the crops and livestock produced by the American farmer. This was only his duty, because the "farm family is the important thing in making and keeping rural America a satisfying home for the human spirit, [and] in developing men and women of great character. . . ."[19] In actual practice, Frank did not make many changes in the magazine. As under the previous editor, the chief offerings were bland short stories and rudimentary articles about farming. There was, however, a marked shift in editorial policy. In almost every issue Frank either directly or indirectly attacked the New Deal's farm policy. In typical fashion he said, "The blunt truth is that —except as a justified means of meeting an emergency— there is neither rhyme nor reason in the fantastic notion that we can bring the Abundant Life to American millions by putting our productive genius in chains, by producing less and charging more. . . . *If we could stop all activity in the United States for just thirty minutes and if every literate American would stand still for these thirty minutes and think this business over, the unbelievable insanity of trying to arrive at a life of abundance through legislating for scarcity would be laughed out of court.* . . . You can surround it with beautiful words. You can call it social-minded, liberal, progressive, but it remains, when seriously considered as a permanent policy, illiberal, unprogressive, reactionary."[20]

As a business venture *Rural Progress* was a disastrous failure, losing $96,000 in one quarter alone. The periodical's doom became a virtual certainty in May, 1938, when it received adverse publicity during the course of a United States Senate investigation of lobbying activities. Two Democratic senators noted the heavy losses, the names of the stockholders, the free distribution, and the anti-New Deal editorial policy. They claimed without positive proof that the publication's real purpose was to promote Frank's political ambitions. Senator Louis B. Schwellenback of Washington thundered, "We don't intend to let you use this as a forum for the Republican party," and Senator Sherman Minton of Indiana dismissed *Rural Progress* as a "propaganda magazine." Frank replied to the charges by accusing the committee members of engaging in "a carefully laid campaign of terror and intimidation against the newspapers and magazines of this country which dare criticize, or even discuss objectively, the policies and activities of the New Deal." Minton retorted, "We're only trying to let the people know where this propaganda is coming from."[21] The investigation and Frank's statement distressed his backers. For example, George Rumely complained to Frank, "*Rural Progress* may have been seriously damaged by this. If advertisers were frightened away, the damage might be irreparable. . . . I think your position would have been immeasurably stronger, so far as advertising and future financial support is concerned had you taken a firm stand of absolute refusal to allow your constitutional rights to be impaired."[22] Frank disagreed, but losses continued to mount.

The periodical struggled along throughout 1938, appeared at increasingly infrequent intervals, and suspended publication in the summer of 1939. A year later Frank made a desperate attempt to resume publication. He proposed that the Republican National Committee secretly contribute $100,000 to publish the magazine in the months immediately prior to the 1940 election. Frank claimed that *Rural Progress* could disseminate anti-New Deal propaganda more effectively than the methods normally used by the party. "It would provide a more permanent and dependable medium for distributing this information to the public than would be the case if such information went out as strictly campaign documents because the magazine has been . . . going out into these farm and rural homes for four and one-half years," he said. "Attention is called to the fact that the publication functioned during the campaign of 1938, with plenty of evidence in the files to indicate its substantial effect upon the general results in the states covered."[23] The National Committee rejected his offer and the magazine was never published again.

Frank felt free to make the offer because he was already closely associated with the Republican party. Since January, 1938, he had been the chairman of a special policy-making group called the Republican Program Committee (RPC), which was to write a statement of party principles intended to guide the platform committee at the 1940 Republican National Convention. Former President Hoover had persuaded Frank to head the RPC. "I was delighted to see the attitude you have taken about my proposals for the Republican party," Hoover had written Frank on October 2, 1937. "What I proposed was that a committee of some twenty to fifty distinguished men should be set up who would explore the entire reorientation of this country and who would outline an affirmative body of principles and methods."[24]

Frank took a rather curious attitude toward the committee. He indicated to John Hamilton, the chairman of the Republican National Committee, that he considered the committee a nonpartisan body, despite its purpose and sponsorship. "It is not the business of this commission to write platforms for the 1938 and 1940 campaigns," he declared. "It is not the business of this commission to promote the candidacy of anyone for any office. This special commission is outside the normal day-to-day operation of the political machinery of the party. . . . Since office-holders are not in its membership this commission is a body of laymen asked to devote themselves behind the line of formal party action to a study of the extraordinarily grave social and economic difficulties that now confront the nation. . . . It will seek to play its full part in a sincere, open minded, responsible search for the principles and lines of national action that will keep America a going concern—with its business, its industry, and its agriculture ministering effectively to the human needs of the whole people—and insure a way of life congenial to the American Spirit."[25]

Under Frank's direction the committee, an unwieldly organization of over two hundred people residing in all parts of the country, struggled along for over two years with no discernible signs of progress. At times Frank seemed more intent upon collecting data and holding meetings than he did upon submitting a final report. He ignored Hamilton's pointed suggestion that a long delay might impair the chances of the Republican party in the 1940 elections.[26] Evidently,

Frank wanted to delay the committee's report until shortly before the 1940 Republican National Convention assembled to select its presidential nominee.

Frank's dilatoriness may have been part of his strategy to secure the nomination for himself. As he was well aware, no one had yet appeared to rally the Republican hosts following the party's disastrous defeat in the 1936 elections. Under the circumstances, the business leaders who played such an important part in financing Republican presidential campaigns were in an even stronger position than usual to select the party's standard-bearer. Frank concluded that these conditions favored his own candidacy. He was known to and respected by many Republican businessmen, and he believed that if his Republican Program Committee issued its report at just the right time, and if it had a significant impact on party leaders, it was not inconceivable that he might be offered the presidential nomination.

Finally, in March, 1940, Frank distributed *A Program for a Dynamic America* to the press and to fifty thousand of the party faithful. "In this document, the Program Committee undertakes to reflect its analysis of the philosophy, policies, and actual results of the present administration and to throw into contrast thereto what, in its judgment, should be the guiding principles of national policy for dealing with the problem of getting our national economy into sustained high gear so that we can realize full employment of our men, our money, and our materials, a progressive rise in our living standards, and an increased security for our people," Frank wrote in the foreword. "Long-range consideration of national policy is made doubly difficult today by the drastic dislocations in Europe and the Far East and by the conflicting political and economic trends which are paralyzing so much of the world's life. Unless by sheer act of will we prevent it, this abnormal world situation is likely to distort our judgment and divert our attention from those basic issues of domestic policy which finally will make or break us as a people."[27] The program proposed by the RPC called for a "watered down" New Deal without some of the bureaucratic controls of the Roosevelt administration. Unfortunately for Frank's ambitions, the report had little impact inside the party and failed to generate even the slightest grassroots sentiment in favor of Frank's nomination.

Frank attempted to answer charges that the report was too mild by stating, "It is a conservative document, but not in the sense of believing that nothing must ever happen for the first time."[28] If he hoped that the report would make him "presidential timber," it was in vain. He was relegated to a minor role on the platform committee at the Philadelphia convention, and even his business acquaintances dismissed him as a contender for the nomination. Instead, they supported Wendell Willkie, who was, ironically, a distant relative of Harold Wilkie, the president of the Board of Regents which had ended Frank's tenure at the University of Wisconsin. On the night of the balloting Frank listened as carefully organized groups in the balcony chanted "We want Willkie! We want Willkie!"

Following the convention Frank returned to Wisconsin, intent on seeking the Republican nomination for the United States Senate. He did so knowing that the Republican organization in the state had already endorsed another candidate for the office, and that the nomination could be won only by winning a stiff, uphill fight in the primary election. The failure of *A Program for a Dynamic America* to make an impact and events that transpired in Philadelphia convinced Frank that he had to participate actively in politics and demonstrate his "vote getting" potential if he was to get a chance to reside in the White House. Frank thought that he could win the primary. Whether or not he believed he could unseat Senator Robert La Follette, Jr., in the general election is uncertain. To be sure, the Progressives had lost to a Republican candidate in the gubernatorial election in 1938, and some observers felt that La Follette would have difficulty holding his Senate seat in 1940. On the other hand, the La Follette name held an undeniable attraction for the voters of Wisconsin. Possibly Frank believed that it would be enough to make a respectable race against such a formidable foe.

Frank announced his candidacy for the senatorial nomination on July 26, 1940, only five days before the deadline for filing. To have his name appear on the ballot he needed the signature of fifteen thousand eligible voters. His task was complicated by a requirement that he obtain the names of at least one per cent of the electorate in each of the state's seventy-one counties. He established headquarters in a tiny room in a Madison hotel and collected a staff consisting entirely of volunteers. "There wasn't any money in sight," noted a reporter, "and the volunteers were busy buying stamps and paying off messenger boys out of their own pockets."[29] But Frank's underdog position captured the imagination of the public, and soon nomination papers began pouring in from around the state. Battling the clock, he filed with less than two hours to spare. Afterwards, he raced to build an organization, to distribute publicity information, and to plan a campaign schedule. Finally there was the campaign itself —the hurried trips, the dozens of speeches, the crowds he loved so well, and at the end grinding brakes, screeching tires, and death on the road to Green Bay.

Thus, suddenly and shockingly, ended the career of a man who came close to reaching commanding heights. His life was the story of what might have been. It was the story of a self-confident and articulate youth from a small Missouri hamlet who rose to become a national figure and the head of a major university. In retrospect he made two grave mistakes. One was accepting the presidency of the University of Wisconsin. Had he remained in New York, in a field which seemed suited to his talents, he might have made a substantial intellectual contribution to American thought as an editor. His second mistake was to remain in the University presidency after his administration had lost the confidence of the faculty and had incurred the animosity of the state's political leaders. He should have known better. As he once said, "For the normal run of mankind, two things constitute the anatomy of failure: first, the selection of the wrong career in the beginning, second, staying in the wrong career after the mistake has been found out."[30]

Glenn Frank had been his own best publicist, and once he was gone he was quickly forgotten. This was unfortunate. He had been at times a shrewd observer of the American scene. Some of his predictions about the future came to pass, and better than many of his contemporaries he stated for popular consumption the problems of the machine age. Yet in the end there remained only the unfulfilled promise and the long, somehow wistful boast of his headstone: "A Devoted Son, Husband, Father, Patriot. A Great Scholar, Orator, Editor, Educator. 'Great as Writer, Educator, But Greater as a Man.'"

NOTES TO THE TEXT

CHAPTER I

[1] The other candidates were Fred H. Clausen, a manufacturer of farm implements; John P. Koehler, former Milwaukee Health commissioner; Michael Elberlein, an attorney; William Maas, former secretary to Governor Julius Heil; Reuben W. Peterson, chairman of the Wisconsin Public Service Commission; and Walter B. Chilsen, a newspaper publisher. *Milwaukee Journal,* September 18, 1940.

[2] "Glenn Frank for U. S. Senator, Itinerary Sheet No. 25, September 15, 1940," and "Notes Found on Glenn Frank's body," in the Glenn Frank Papers at Northwest Missouri State Teachers College. Hereinafter cited as Frank Papers. For detailed information on the events leading up to and the circumstances of the accident see the *Wisconsin State Journal* (Madison), September 16, 17, 1940. All Wisconsin newspapers covered the campaign. The most inclusive coverage was given by the *Wisconsin State Journal,* the *Capital Times* (Madison), the *Milwaukee Journal,* and the *Milwaukee Sentinel.* The quotations from Frank's campaign speeches are from the *Wisconsin State Journal,* September 10, 1940, and the *Milwaukee Journal,* September 12, 1940.

[3] Obituaries appeared in many places. Long and detailed ones can be found in the *Capital Times* and the *Wisconsin State Journal* for September 16, 1940, plus the *Milwaukee Journal* of the same date. See also the *New York Times,* September 16, 1940.

[4] John Hicks, who had known Glenn Frank since they were students together at Northwestern University, gave a moving eulogy before the Madison Literary Society. John Hicks, "Draft of Speech to Madison Literary Society," October 6, 1940, in the John Hicks Papers on Glenn Frank at the State Historical Society of Wisconsin. Hereinafter cited as Hicks Papers. Hicks, a professor of history in the University of Wisconsin, later became dean of the University of California Graduate School. A series of tributes is contained in *In Appreciation of Glenn Frank: Proceedings of the First Annual Wisconsin X Club Banquet Upon the Occasion of the Presentation of the*

Glenn Frank Memorial Portrait to the University of Wisconsin (Madison, June 20, 1941).

[5] Green Top, and the surrounding countryside at the time of Frank's birth, is described in *History of Adair, Sullivan, Putnam and Schuyler Counties, Missouri* (Chicago, 1888). See also Eugene Violette, *History of Adair County* (Kirksville, Missouri, 1911).

[6] Glenn Frank, editorial entitled "The Audience Habit," December 28, 1925, in the Frank Papers. The date given here and in subsequent places is the release date. Frank's columns, which he preferred to call editorials, appeared five days a week in over sixty newspapers, including the *Chicago Daily News*, the *New York World*, and the *San Francisco Bulletin*, between the fall of 1925 and the spring of 1938. On numerous occasions he emphasized the value of his Missouri heritage.

[7] Glenn Frank, editorials entitled "Portrait of a Father," September 19, 1934, and "Tribute to a Mother," June 6, 1932, in the Frank Papers. Frank expressed similar thoughts about his mother in a letter to Hazel Beman, April 25, 1936, in Presidents of the University, General Correspondence, Series 4/11/1, in the University of Wisconsin Archives. Hereinafter cited as President's Papers. Frank did not write extensively about either of his parents. Both were of Scotch-Irish and Scotch descent. Their parents had migrated to Missouri following the War of 1812 to claim bounty lands. Mrs. Glenn Frank to John Hicks, January 31, 1956, in the Hicks Papers.

[8] *Wisconsin State Journal*, July 1, 1928, contains an interview with Claude Frank, then a barber in Green Top. Another brother, William, who taught Frank for a term in grade school, read law, became a noted Missouri lawyer, and for several years was Chief Justice of the Missouri State Supreme Court.

[9] Interview with a Green Top neighbor of the Frank family, *ibid.*, August 6, 1933.

[10] *Ibid.*, July 1, 1928, September 16, 1940.

[11] "Local Preacher's License," December 2, 1903, in the Frank Papers. It was common practice for Methodist Conferences in predominately rural areas with few ordained ministers to use Local Preachers in their place. Under Missouri law, Local Preachers could perform marriages.

[12] Frank to Mrs. Gordon Frank, no date, probably 1907 or 1908, in the Frank Papers.

[13] *Kirksville Express*, quoted in *Glenn Frank, Northwestern University, Lecturer of Purpose* (Des Moines, 1913).

[14] Glenville Kleiser, *The World's Great Sermons* (10 volumes, New York, 1908); R. A. Torrey, *Revival Addresses* (Chicago, New York, and Toronto, 1903); T. De Witt Talmadge, *Selected Sermons* (19 volumes, New York, 1900); Alexander Maclaren, *Expositions of Holy Scripture* (12 volumes, New York, 1906). See also *Wisconsin State Journal*, May 31, 1925.

[15] "Permanent Card of Glenn Frank," in the Registrar's Office, at Northeast Missouri State Teachers College.

[16] *The Echo*, 4:40–43 (Kirksville, 1906). A trip that Frank took to St. Joseph, Missouri, to attend a YMCA meeting is recounted in E. A. Funkhouser to Frank, September 30, 1925, in the President's Papers.

[17] *Wisconsin State Journal*, May 31, 1925; photograph, 1907 or 1908, in the Frank Papers. In the photograph Frank is shown with two other evangelists standing in front of their meeting tent. Many years later a man who heard

Frank preach on the circuit wrote to him: "Though I do not remember any-thing that you said I can still see the sporty cloth top shoes you wore." Claude Sprouce to Frank, September 24, 1928, in the President's Papers.
    [18] Glenn Frank, editorial entitled "Billy Sunday Passes," November 14, 1935, in the Frank Papers. Frank also impressed Sunday. He used some of Frank's material for his sermons, followed his subsequent career, and wrote him a cordial letter after he became president of the University of Wisconsin. "Some time when you want Billy Sunday to come up there and address the students I believe maybe I can arrange to have him do it. . . . I hope to see you before long, and renew the friendship that means very much to me," Sunday wrote. Frank did not invite Sunday to Madison, nor did they meet again. William Sunday to Frank, May 23, 1925, in the Frank Papers. See also William McLoughlin, Jr., *Billy Sunday was His Real Name* (Chicago, 1955), 166.

CHAPTER II

[1] Frank told about his admission difficulties in the *Daily Cardinal* (Madison), December 2, 1931. The Registrar's Office of Northwestern University substantiated his account, December 28, 1961. See also *Wisconsin State Journal*, September 16, 1940.
    [2] The school newspaper, the *Daily Northwestern* (Evanston), 1910–1912, covers the day-by-day activities of the University for the period in which Frank was a student. See also various summaries of progress on the campus in the *Northwestern University Bulletin Series*, 1910–1912, and the school annual, the *Syllabus*, for the same years.
    [3] Horace Garrett to James Alton James, April 18, 1941; James T. Haviland to James Alton James, April 8, 1941, in the James Alton James Papers in the Northwestern University Archives. James, a professor at Northwestern at the time Frank was a student, solicited the letters for help in preparing a tribute to Frank, contained in James Alton James, "Glenn Frank and His Relationship to Northwestern University," in *In Appreciation of Glenn Frank.*
    [4] *Syllabus* (Evanston, 1912), 25, 88; *Daily Northwestern,* October 12, 1911; *Daily Cardinal,* January 17, 1929; James, "Glenn Frank and His Relationship to Northwestern University."
    [5] *Daily Northwestern,* January 13, 1912.
    [6] "Advertising Talks, Three T's," in the *Northwestern Magazine,* 9:12 (October, 1911).
    [7] *Daily Northwestern,* October 13, 1911.
    [8] Frank wrote the articles under the name "I. G. Frank" for reasons he never explained. Frank, "Maurice Maeterlinck," 9:1 (October, 1911); "Gilbert K. Chesterton," 9:53 (November, 1911); "George Bernard Shaw," 9:105 (December, 1911); "Edmond Rostand," 9:151 (January, 1912); "Henrik Ibsen," 9:205 (February, 1912); "Leo Tolstoy," 9:263 (March, 1912); "Louis Steven-

son," 9:305 (April, 1912); "Mr. Roosevelt's Philosophy of Life," 9:355 (May, 1912), all in the *Northwestern Magazine.*

[9] James, "Glenn Frank and His Relationship to Northwestern University."

[10] John Hicks, "Draft of Speech to Madison Literary Society," October 6, 1940, in the Hicks Papers.

[11] *Daily Northwestern,* November 9, 1911.

[12] *Ibid.,* May 4, 1912; "Morals and Machinery, or a Public Age with a Private Conscience, Northern Oratorical League Oration for 1912, Northwestern University," in the Frank Papers.

[13] *Glenn Frank, Northwestern University, Lecturer of Purpose* (Des Moines, 1913) advertises Frank's prowess as a platform lecturer. Further information is contained in the *Wisconsin State Journal,* September 16, 1940; the *Daily Cardinal,* December 2, 1931. See also Beuhlah Buck Fogleman to Frank, August 27, 1927; Frank to G. W. Ray, February 4, 1927, in the President's Papers.

[14] *Religion and Modern Life: Huron Chautauqua Assembly* (Huron, South Dakota, 1911); Huron, South Dakota, and Hamilton, Missouri, Press Reports, quoted in *Glenn Frank of Northwestern University, The Modern Problem Lecturer* (Des Moines, 1912).

[15] *Wisconsin State Journal,* September 21, 1927, contains quotations from a speech by Frank in which he discussed his college days. See also Frank to George Morton, June 2, 1926; Frank to Rudolph Ericson, June 29, 1926, in President's Papers. For Frank's grades, see "Record of Work Completed, Northwestern University, Second Semester, 1910–1911," in the Frank Papers. Frank's official transcript is closed.

[16] Northwestern University News Release, May 23, 1925, in the Northwestern University Archives; James, "Glenn Frank and His Relationship to Northwestern University."

[17] Frank to Mr. and Mrs. Gordon Frank, December 11, 1911, in the Frank Papers.

[18] *Daily Northwestern,* October 1, 1912; "The Appointment of Glenn Frank as Alumni Secretary of the University," in the *Northwestern University Bulletin,* 8:7 (October 18, 1912).

[19] Abram Harris to Frank, June 14, 1912, in the Abram Harris Papers in the Northwestern University Archives.

[20] "Editor's Comments," in the *Alumni Journal Northwestern University Bulletin,* 15:31 (May 7, 1915). For information on how Frank broadened the operations of his office, see James, "Glenn Frank and His Relationship to Northwestern University"; Northwestern *Alumni News,* October, 1940; "Minutes of the Meeting of Alumni Association," October 16, 1914, February 27, 1915, in the Northwestern University Archives; *Northwestern University President's Report,* 1912–1913; *Daily Northwestern,* May 14, 1914, December 11, 1915. Enrollment increased by about three hundred students while Frank was Alumni Secretary.

[21] "Report of the Alumni Secretary," in the *Alumni News Letter, Northwestern University Bulletin,* 15:18 (February 19, 1915). See also the *Daily Northwestern,* March 20, October 9, 1913, March 26, September 25, 1914.

[22] "Gordon Frank's Financial Records," in the Frank Papers.

CHAPTER III

[1] Gerald W. Johnson, *Liberal's Progress* (New York, 1948), 1–77; J. H. Willits, "Arbitration Plan of William Filene's Sons Company," in the *Annals of the American Academy*, 69:205–207 (January, 1917).

[2] "Edward A. Filene," in the *National Cyclopaedia of American Biography* (Volume A, current, New York, 1926), 319–320. See also obituaries in the *New York Times* and the *New York Herald Tribune*, September 27, 1937.

[3] Hamilton Holt, closely associated with Filene in the League to Enforce Peace, discusses his personality in "Glenn Frank," in *In Appreciation of Glenn Frank*. For an especially vicious attack on Filene's motives, see Ernest Meyer, "Glenn Frank: Journalist on Parole," in the *American Mercury*, 31:150 (January, 1934).

[4] Walter Dill Scott, who succeeded Abram Harris as president of Northwestern University, explained his part in Frank's selection as Filene's assistant in a *Northwestern University News Release*, May 23, 1925.

[5] Holt, "Glenn Frank," details Frank's role in the League to Enforce Peace. See also Ruhl J. Bartlett, *The League to Enforce Peace* (Chapel Hill, 1944). Frank was not called into service, but he said he would have been if hostilities had lasted six months longer. Glenn Frank to Edith Stephenson, April 21, 1925, in the Glenn Frank Papers.

[6] Glenn Frank to Mrs. Glenn Frank, March 21, 1918, in the Frank Papers.

[7] Lothrop Stoddard and Glenn Frank, *Stakes in the War* (New York, 1918), vii. Edward Filene to Newton Baker, Woodrow Wilson, Henry Ford, and others, October 14, 1918, and unlabeled notebook of correspondence to Edward Filene concerning *Stakes in the War*, 1919, in the Frank Papers. Frank received $1,291.48 royalties during 1919. Glenn Frank, "Work Sheet for New York State Income Tax, 1919," in *ibid*. Stoddard wrote frequent letters to Frank in the 1920's, none of which Frank answered. For Stoddard's views on race, see Lothrop Stoddard, *The Rising Tide of Color* (New York, 1920).

[8] Glenn Frank, *The Politics of Industry* (New York, 1919).

[9] Glenn Frank to Mary Smith, February 11, 1916, in the Frank Papers. See also Glenn Frank to Mary Smith, February [?], March [?], 1916, in *ibid*. Mary Frank tells about how she and Glenn were childhood sweethearts in Mrs. Glenn Frank to John Hicks, January 31, 1956, in the Hicks Papers.

[10] Mrs. Glenn Frank's father to Mrs. Glenn Frank, November 13, 1918, in the Frank Papers; *St. Louis Post Dispatch*, June 3, 1917.

[11] Aunt Agnes to Florence, probably 1918, in the Frank Papers; Emil B. Fry, "Glenn Frank, Jr.," in *In Appreciation of Glenn Frank*. Frank wrote his parents about his married life in Frank to Mr. and Mrs. Gordon Frank, August 23, 1918, in the Frank Papers. See also Mrs. Glenn Frank to John Hicks in the Hicks Papers. Frank wanted his son to have every possible educational advantage, and he enrolled him in Groton School for the 1932 term not long after his birth. Lawrence Andrews to Glenn Frank, October 29, 1919, in the Frank Papers.

[12] Frank discussed Filene and his ideas in *The Politics of Industry* (New York, 1919), 184–190. Frank and Filene remained friendly over the years. Filene strongly recommended Frank for the presidency of the University of Wisconsin in 1925. In the early 1930's Frank said that Filene possessed a "rare genius for abstract sympathy," that he was a rich man endowed with a sense of trusteeship, and that knowing him was an indelible experience. Glenn Frank, *Thunder and Dawn* (New York, 1932), 232.

CHAPTER IV

[1] The history of the *Century Magazine* is sketched in Theodore Peterson, *Magazines in the Twentieth Century* (Urbana, 1956), 136–137.

[2] Glenn Frank to Mrs. Glenn Frank [?], 1919, in the Frank Papers.

[3] Glenn Frank to Mrs. Glenn Frank [?], 1919, in *ibid.*

[4] "Memo, Re adoption by the *Century* of a Special editorial plan for handling the problem of Reconstruction, 1919," and "Memo, Conference between Mr. Schuster and Mr. Frank regarding a proposed Magazine on Reconstruction, 1919," in *ibid.*

[5] W. Morgan Schuster, in the *Century Magazine*, 101:678 (April, 1921).

[6] Glenn Frank to Zona Gale, April 17, 1925, in the Frank Papers.

[7] Frank told Hamlin Garland about his need for literary contacts at a private party. Hamlin Garland, *My Friendly Contemporaries* (New York, 1932), 344. Garland said that Frank "is handsome, clear eyed, and aspiring and will readily take on culture." The changes that Frank made in the *Century* are discussed in Holt, "Glenn Frank," and Peterson, *Magazines in the Twentieth Century*, 137. Frank tells how he enjoyed introducing new talent as editor in Glenn Frank to George Cady, December 1, 1933, in the President's Papers. Wiggam credited Frank with making him a best-selling writer in the *Daily Cardinal*, October 31, 1928. Hindus expressed his relief in a letter to Mrs. Glenn Frank, mentioned in Mrs. Glenn Frank to John Hicks, January 31, 1956, in the Hicks Papers. See also Eugene Debs to Glenn Frank, March 30, 1922, in the Frank Papers. One of Frank's brothers, Claude, did not care for the *Century*. He is quoted as saying, "Glenn offered to send it to me and he did send a couple of copies but I told him never mind because I didn't read it anyway." *Wisconsin State Journal*, July 1, 1928.

[8] Glenn Frank, "Americanism: Selective or Sentimental," in the *Century Magazine*, 104:478 (August, 1922).

[9] Glenn Frank, "The Wages of Complexity," 107:317–320 (December, 1923); "The Market Value of Philosophers," 107:634 (February, 1924); "Patriotism and Pacifism," 108:425 (July, 1924), all in the *Century Magazine*.

[10] Glenn Frank, "A Reform to End Reforms," 108:861 (October, 1924); "Is States' Rights a Dead Issue?" 109:842 (April, 1924), all in the *Century Magazine*.

[11] Glenn Frank, *An American Looks at His World* (New York, 1925).

[12] Glenn Frank to Louis Alber, May 5, 1924, in the Frank Papers. Information on Frank's honorariums can be found in Louis Alber to Glenn Frank,

October 11, 1924, in *ibid.* John Hicks, who heard Frank speak in 1924 at the University of Nebraska, recalled, "He spoke without notes or manuscripts as was his custom at the time and for an hour he held that huge audience in the hollow of his hand." John Hicks, "Draft of speech to Madison Literary Society," in the Hicks Papers.

[13] For information on Frank's life and friends in New York, see Glenn Frank to Alkyne Ireland, January 8, 1926, in the President's Papers; also Ray Howard to Frank, October 1, 1923, Frank to Edward Filene, April 7, 1925, Bernard Baruch to Frank, June 19, 1925, and Franklin Roosevelt to Frank, August 12, 1924, all in the Frank Papers. On Frank's role as an adviser to William McAdoo, see William McAdoo to Frank, June 2, 1923, and Frank to William McAdoo, June 12, 1923, in *ibid.* The observations of Norman Thomas are based on the author's interview with Norman Thomas, November 13, 1962.

CHAPTER V

[1] Glenn Frank to Edward Filene, April 7, 1925, in the Frank Papers. The basic source for information about the history of the University of Wisconsin is Merle Curti and Vernon Carstensen, *The University of Wisconsin, 1848–1925* (2 volumes, Madison, 1949). It is summarized in *The University of Wisconsin History Digest, A Land-Grant Centennial Publication* (Madison, 1962).

[2] For sketches of individual Regents, see the *Dictionary of Wisconsin Biography* (Madison, 1960). Zona Gale discussed the composition of the Board in Zona Gale to Frank, May 14, 1925, in the Frank Papers.

[3] Curti and Carstensen, *The University of Wisconsin,* 2:157. Senator La Follette's role was further complicated by his final illness in the spring of 1925. He died on June 18, 1925.

[4] *Wisconsin State Journal,* January 25, 1925; *Boston Transcript,* January 26, 1925.

[5] Copy of Letter from Roscoe Pound to John Callahan, January 27, 1925, in the Theodore Kronshage Papers at the State Historical Society of Wisconsin. Hereinafter cited as the Kronshage Papers. The letter also appears in George Sellery, *Some Ferments at the University of Wisconsin, Memories and Reflections* (Madison, 1960), 85–86.

[6] John Callahan to Edward Filene, June 10, 1924, in the Michael Olbrich Papers at the State Historical Society of Wisconsin. Hereinafter cited as the Olbrich Papers.

[7] Edward Filene to John Callahan, October 8, 1924, in *ibid.* In the spring of 1925 Olbrich served as secretary of the nominating committee, which explains how he ended up with some of Callahan's correspondence.

[8] Zona Gale's biographer tells a different story. He states that following the Pound fiasco, Zona and Callahan went on to New York and that she, Callahan, and Frank were riding together when she impulsively said, "Why not Glenn Frank for the President of the University of Wisconsin?" August

Derleth, *Still Small Voice: The Biography of Zona Gale* (New York, 1940), 167–168.

[9] Frank to Zona Gale, April 7, 1925, in the Frank Papers.

[10] Zona Gale to Frank, April 14, 1925, in *ibid.*

[11] Frank to Zona Gale, April 17, 1925, in *ibid.*

[12] Walter Dill Scott to John Callahan, May 5, 1925, and Edward Filene to John Callahan, May 5, 1925, in the Olbrich Papers; also Zona Gale to Frank, May 10, 1925, in the Frank Papers. The committee did not keep a formal record of its proceedings. Abram Harris, president of Northwestern University when Frank was alumni secretary, sent a letter that arrived too late to be considered. Harris said, "He is a clean man in thought and action, sincere and friendly. He is progressive, but not given to denunciation. I am confident that if elected he will win friends among business men, and political men. He is in perfect health, carries burdens without complaining; is frank and good tempered. He is happily married to a charming woman." Abram Harris to Theodore Kronshage, May 11, 1925, in the Olbrich Papers.

[13] Zona Gale to Frank, May 14, 1925, in the Frank Papers. This is a very revealing letter. The Board of Regents kept no formal record. The Board's secretary explained why in a letter to Harold Wilkie, president of the Board, on December 29, 1936: "My impression is that on that date [May 13, 1925], the Regents were contacted and that a unanimous approval of the appointment was obtained; that no record was made at the time as they probably wished to keep it out of the papers until negotiations were completed." The letter is in Board of Regents, Secretary, Miscellaneous File, Series 1/1/2, in the University of Wisconsin Archives. Hereinafter cited as Regents' Miscellaneous File. As usually happens, the Frank appointment was quickly leaked to the press. See *Wisconsin State Journal*, May 13, 1925. For the record, Frank's appointment was officially approved by the Board at their next regularly scheduled meeting. Record "L," June 22, 1925, in Board of Regents, Minutes, Series 1/1/1, in the University of Wisconsin Archives.

[14] Zona Gale to Frank, May 14, 1925, in the Frank Papers. Frank did not make Kronshage assistant to the president.

[15] Arnold Hall to Frank, May 12, 1925, in *ibid.* The date of the letter is worth noting, because it is dated the day before the Regents' meeting. Either it was a simple mistake or Hall had advance knowledge.

[16] "Memorandum of Agreement Between the Undersigned Committee of the Board of Regents of the University of Wisconsin and Glenn Frank," no date, probably May 20, 1925, in Regents' Miscellaneous File.

[17] *Wisconsin State Journal*, May 20, 1925.

[18] For the reaction of some of Frank's friends in New York, see Alfred Smith to Frank, May 23, 1925; Fannie Hurst to Frank, May 23, 1925; and Cornelius Vanderbilt to Frank, May 21, 1925, in the Frank Papers. Editorials on Frank's selection appeared in *Wisconsin State Journal*, May 21, 1925; *Capital Times*, May 23, 1925; *Milwaukee Journal*, May 21, 1925. Ross' statement is in *Wisconsin State Journal*, May 25, 1925.

[19] Edward Birge to Frank, May 20, 1925, in the Frank Papers, and Sellery, *Some Ferments at Wisconsin*, 86. Twelve years later, Frank claimed that he was told by a member of the La Follette family (who denied the story),

on the day he accepted the presidency, that the action of the Board did not reflect the Senator's wishes.

[20] *Wisconsin State Journal,* May 26, 1925.

[21] *Ibid.,* May 27, 1925.

CHAPTER VI

[1] *Capital Times,* September 1, 1925; *Wisconsin State Journal,* September 2, 1925.

[2] Glenn Frank, *An American Looks at His World* (New York, 1923), 198–201; Glenn Frank, "State Universities in State Politics," in the *Century Magazine,* 109:121–124 (May, 1925).

[3] *Wisconsin State Journal,* September 13, 1925; *Capital Times,* September 4, 1925.

[4] *Chicago Daily News,* September 19, 1925. See also *Wisconsin State Journal,* September 6, 25, 1925, and *Capital Times,* September 3, 1925.

[5] Frank to William Van Loon, January 8, 1926, in the President's Papers.

[6] Frank described his approach in an interview published in *Wisconsin State Journal,* June 20, 1926.

[7] Sellery, *Some Ferments at Wisconsin,* 35. Sellery was apparently the only person connected with the University who saw the reports. Frank probably destroyed them, because of the nature of their contents.

[8] See "Unfinished Notes of Presidential Talk, Summer, 1927, Visitors"; Frank to Louis Alber, September 26, 1925; Frank to Edward Birge, June 11, 1925; "Minutes of Faculty Meeting," October 5, 1925, in the President's Papers; *Wisconsin State Journal,* November 3, 1925.

[9] The fund-raising controversy is discussed in detail in Curti and Carstensen, *The University of Wisconsin,* 2:223–228.

[10] Zona Gale to Frank, July 5, 1925, and William Olbrich to Frank, August 11, 1925, in the Frank Papers.

[11] Curti and Carstensen, *The University of Wisconsin,* 2:228–229.

[12] *Wisconsin State Journal,* October 8, 1925; *Capital Times,* November 9, 1925.

[13] Curti and Carstensen, *The University of Wisconsin,* 2:230–232.

[14] Frank to Albert Wiggam, January 8, 1926, in the President's Papers.

[15] Frank to Alfred Lloyd, February 7, 1926, in the Frank Papers.

[16] Frank to Alexander Meiklejohn, December 10, 1925, in the President's Papers; Alexander Meiklejohn, "A New College, Notes on Next Steps in Higher Education," in the *Century Magazine* (January, 1925). For information on Meiklejohn's career, see the *Milwaukee Journal,* June 3, 1962.

[17] "Address to Faculty," March 1, 1926, in the President's Papers.

[18] Sellery, *Some Ferments at Wisconsin,* 14.

[19] *Wisconsin State Journal,* June 21, 1926.

CHAPTER VII

[1] Horace Ellis to Frank, October 26, 1925, and Frank Starbuck to Frank, December 7, 1925, in the President's Papers. *Wisconsin State Journal,* May 1, 1927; Frank to Henry Luce, January 6, 1925, in the Frank Papers. *Daily Cardinal,* January 4, 1929; *Newark Star-Eagle,* November 23, 1925; August Derleth, *Still Small Voice,* 232; Meyer, "Glenn Frank: Journalist on Parole."

[2] "Unfinished Notes of Presidential Talk, Summer, 1927, Visitors," in the President's Papers. The *Chicago Tribune,* November 9, 22, 1927, contains editorials criticizing the University for supposedly fostering pacifism. For Frank's reply, see the *Capital Times,* November 24, 1927. The controversy over the Russell visit is summarized in the *Wisconsin State Journal,* February 15, 1928. Frank received over one hundred letters applauding his stand. Some "liberals," however, wrote him very critical letters. Frank replied, "But, it seems an unhappy fact that unless a man agrees in every minute detail with his liberal colleagues, some of them temporarily adjourn their own philosophy of tolerance and a temperate weighing of all the evidence and decline to give him any credit either for sincerity or for honesty." Frank to several people, February, 1929, in the President's Papers.

[3] *Wisconsin State Journal,* May 22, 1927.

[4] The quotations from Frank speeches are from *ibid.,* March 24, December 9, 1927; *Daily Cardinal,* February 12, 1927, May 7, October 15, 1929; *Milwaukee Sentinel,* January 18, 1926; and *Oshkosh Northwestern,* April 22, 1929.

[5] Glenn Frank, editorial entitled "Resetting the Clocks," August 27, 1928, in the Frank Papers. See also Glenn Frank, editorials entitled "The Cost of Liberty," May 5, 1926, "We Need Philosophers," October 23, 1926, and "The Peril of the Big," August 1, 1927, in *ibid.*

[6] Frank's highly popular prayer was reprinted in many places, such as the *Milwaukee Journal,* February 29, 1928. See also Glenn Frank, "Eliot, Iconoclast and Builder," in the *Nation,* 123:294 (September 29, 1926); *Capital Times,* March 22, 1926; *Daily Cardinal,* April 26, 1927, December 12, 1929; Frank to Kate Valentine, April 5, 1928, in the President's Papers; *Wisconsin State Journal,* December 15, 1928; and Frank, editorial entitled "Portrait of a Gifted Mind," October 8, 1929, in the Frank Papers.

[7] Walter Dill Scott to Frank, October 9, 1925, in the President's Papers.

[8] Albert Agency advertisements, 1928–1929, in the President's Papers. See also Frank's Secretary to Amy Gordon, May 12, 1925; Frank's Secretary to Max Adelman, July 6, 1926; and Abbie Clark to Frank, March 8, 1926, in *ibid.*

[9] Frank to A. M. Brayton, July 7, 1925, and McClure Syndicate advertisement, "Gems of Thought," 1928, in the Frank Papers; Frank to C. T. Brainerd, July 2, 1928, in the President's Papers. The Regents did not complain about Frank's continuation of his column until well into the 1930's.

[10] Frank to George Mead, June 25, 1930, in the President's Papers. Frank

borrowed money from one of his old Chautauqua acquaintances. Albert Wiggam to Frank, October 11, 1927, in *ibid.*

[11] For examples of the social functions at the Frank residence, see *Wisconsin State Journal,* May 2, 8, August 27, 1927, January 17, 25, 1928, February 6, 1929; *Capital Times,* May 2, 1927; and *Milwaukee Journal,* August 17, 1928. For the way the Franks lived in New York, see Frank to Savoy Hotel, November 28, 1929, in the President's Papers. Frank obtained a living room and two-bedroom suite for "two or three weeks" at $40.00 a day.

[12] Frank to George Creel, November 6, 1926, in the President's Papers. See also Frank to Benjamin Hampton, February 23, 1927; Frank to Robert Adamson, October 25, 1926; Frank to M. H. Krumbine, September 13, 1926; Frank to John Haynes Holmes, June 2, 1928, in *ibid.*

[13] Frank to Stratton D. Brooks, September 22, 1927, in *ibid.*

[14] Glenn Frank editorial entitled "Reading in Office Hours," October 19, 1929, in the Frank Papers. Some people who disapproved of Frank's administration did not think he spent enough time on the job. Dean George Sellery said, "As matters went we of the faculty were at least half inclined to believe the story that Mr. Frank had boasted at a dinner party in Chicago that his presidential duties required only two hours a day." George Sellery, *Some Ferments at Wisconsin,* 88–89.

[15] Frank to Walter Alexander, May 7, 1929, in the President's Papers.

[16] *Milwaukee Journal,* January 30, 1929, contains an excellent account of Frank's lobbying methods.

[17] "Notes for Presentation to 1929 Jt. Finance Committee," in the President's Papers.

[18] Frank to Joseph E. Davies, April 17, 1929, in *ibid.*

[19] *Milwaukee Journal,* January 30, 1929.

[20] *Wisconsin State Journal,* September 21, 1927. See also Sellery, *Some Ferments at Wisconsin,* 9–34; Glenn Frank, "Preliminary Announcement of Experimental College," in the President's Papers; *Milwaukee Journal,* June 3, 1962.

[21] Meiklejohn is quoted in an article in the *Milwaukee Journal,* June 3, 1962. For correspondence relating to Elliot Roosevelt's possible matriculation in the Experimental College, see Franklin Roosevelt to Frank, January 13, April 10, 1930, Frank to Franklin Roosevelt, May 6, 1930, in the President's Papers.

[22] Sellery, *Some Ferments at Wisconsin,* 9–34; *Milwaukee Journal,* June 3, 1962; *Wisconsin State Journal,* March 25, April 20, November 12, 1928, April 20, 1929, February 17, 1932; *Daily Cardinal,* March 8, 1927.

[23] Interview with Mark Ingraham, July 11, 1962. For an example of the problems faced by an instructor, see Walter Agard to Frank, March 16, 1929, in the President's Papers.

[24] Frank to Alexander Meiklejohn, August 11, 1928, in the President's Papers.

[25] *Wisconsin State Journal,* March 9, 1929.

[26] George Sellery to Frank, March 10, 1929, in the Frank Papers.

CHAPTER VIII

[1] For typical observations on social life at the University of Wisconsin in the 1920's, see *Wisconsin State Journal,* February 15, September 14, 1926, March 4, 26, May 28, June 16, 1927, November 10, 1929; for the early 1930's, see *ibid.,* February 7, 1930, September 8, 20, 1931, February 26, September 25, October 4, 1932, and *Capital Times,* January 28, 30, March 13, 1932; for Frank's prediction of an increase in enrollment, see *Wisconsin State Journal,* September 14, 1930.

[2] George Sellery, in *Some Ferments at Wisconsin,* 39, comments on changes caused by the Depression. See also, *Wisconsin State Journal,* October 27, 1932.

[3] Sellery, *Some Ferments at Wisconsin,* 94; *Wisconsin State Journal,* August 6, 1932, January 7, 1933; interview with Mark Ingraham, July 11, 1962; Frank to Oscar Morris, September 7, 1932, in the President's Papers.

[4] Memorandum, Scott Goodnight to Frank, January 15, 1930, in the President's Papers.

[5] William Ellery Leonard to Frank, January 9, 1930, in *ibid.* Leonard's letter appeared in the *Wisconsin State Journal* and *Capital Times,* both for January 17, 1930.

[6] William Ellery Leonard, *The Locomotive God* (New York, 1927).

[7] *Merrill Daily Herald,* January 22, 1930; C. E. Dike to Frank, January 20, 1930, in the President's Papers.

[8] *Wisconsin State Journal,* January 26, 1930.

[9] *Wisconsin State Journal,* May 1, 10, July 12, 1931; copy of letter, "Girl's Mother" to William Ellery Leonard, February 24, 1930, Frank to Committee Members, September 25, 1931, in the President's Papers; *Milwaukee Leader,* September 28, 1932.

[10] Frederick Rosentretter, *The Boundaries of the Campus* (Madison, 1957), 138–145, covers Snell's appointment, tenure, and removal. See also *Wisconsin State Journal,* April 24, 28, 29, May 1, June 7, 1935.

[11] B. D. Evans to H. M. Wilkie, March 7, 1932, in the President's Papers; *Wisconsin State Journal,* April 9, 1932; *Daily Cardinal,* October 17, 1933.

[12] The transcript and aftermath of the Regent's hearing is contained in *Wisconsin State Journal,* December 11, 16, 18, 20, 1935, January 14, 16, 29, February 15, March 1, 10, 1936.

[13] Frank to Frank Graham, April 3, 1935, Frank to Albert Fiedler, April 25, 1936, in the President's Papers; *Wisconsin State Journal,* April 26, December 13, 1935.

[14] Milton Duckett to Frank, March 12, 1932, in the President's Papers. For information on radicalism, see *Wisconsin State Journal,* May 2, 1931, March 30, 1932, May 1, 1933, April 12, 1935.

[15] For Chapple's views, see *Wisconsin State Journal,* November 17, 1931, May 20, 23, 1932; *Daily Cardinal,* November 17, 1931; *Duluth News Tribune,* January 26, 1932; John Chapple, *La Follette Socialism* (Ashland, 1931); John Chapple, *La Follette Road to Socialism* (Ashland, 1935).

[16] "Notes and collected data," spring, 1935, in the William Burnette Papers at the State Historical Society of Wisconsin. Hereinafter cited as the Burnette Papers. For an account of the committee in action, see *Wisconsin State Journal,* April 11, 1935.

[17] "Draft of Special Senate Committee Report, 1935," in the Burnette Papers.

[18] Detailed accounts of the incident can be found in *Daily Cardinal; Capital Times; Milwaukee Journal; Milwaukee Wisconsin News,* all for May 16, 1935. *Wisconsin State Journal,* May 18, 19, 1935, covers the convocation. See also Sellery, *Some Ferments at Wisconsin,* 61–72.

[19] *Wisconsin State Journal,* June 20, 1932; Frank to Myron Hawshaw, June 7, 1935, Myron Hawshaw to Frank, June 10, 1935, in the President's Papers. Hawshaw was then president of the Wisconsin Alumni Association.

[20] Glenn Frank, editorials entitled "Fighting Communism," December 5, 1930, and "Turning the Clock Hands Back," May 25, 1935, in the Frank Papers. *Wisconsin State Journal,* May 13, 1932.

[21] *Daily Cardinal,* January 24, 1931; *Wisconsin State Journal,* April 17, 1930; Sellery, *Some Ferments at Wisconsin,* 54; interview with Mark Ingraham, July 11, 1962; Frank to Owen Young, May 30, 1932, Ernest Gruening to Frank, March 29, 1932, in the Frank Papers.

[22] Sellery, *Some Ferments at Wisconsin,* 38.

[23] *Wisconsin State Journal,* May 14, 1927; Glenn Frank, "Statement for dedication of La Follette Statue in Capitol," no date; Philip La Follette to Frank, April 17, 1927, in the President's Papers; Sellery, *Some Ferments at Wisconsin,* 89.

[24] *Wisconsin State Journal,* December 12, 1930. See also Edward Kremers, "Sketch of Theodore Kronshage," no date, in the Edward Kremers Papers at the State Historical Society of Wisconsin. La Follette may also have been influenced by several faculty members who did not care for Frank's administration, including a close personal friend, Max Otto, a professor of philosophy.

[25] "Toast by Glenn Frank," January 7, 1931, in the President's Papers.

[26] *Wisconsin State Journal,* November 3, 1931, May 2, June 19, 1935; *Daily Cardinal,* February 19, 1931; Transcript, Meeting No. 12, February 9, 1935, in Minutes of the Joint Committee on Finance, Legislative Branch, Joint Committees, Series 7/5/4, at the State Historical Society of Wisconsin. Hereinafter cited as Committee Minutes.

[27] *Wisconsin State Journal,* June 14, 1935. See also Glenn Frank, "The University and the Depression, Statement to Joint Finance Committee," Meeting 11, February 9, 1933, in Committee Minutes.

[28] Meyer, "Glenn Frank: Journalist on Parole."

[29] Frank to Zona Gale, January 4, 1934, in the Frank Papers.

[30] Zona Gale, "Some Achievements of Glenn Frank," in the *American Mercury,* 31:381–383 (March, 1934).

[31] Mark Ingraham to Frank, February 6, 1934, in the Frank Papers; *Wisconsin State Journal,* February 6, 1934.

CHAPTER IX

[1] La Follette reminisced about the Depression period in an interview that appeared in *Capital Times,* December 7, 1959.

[2] Wilkie's version of the conferences can be found in *Wisconsin State Journal*, December 15, 1936, January 6, 7, 1937. See also, Sellery, *Some Ferments at Wisconsin*, 90. Grady claimed that the governor declared that a majority of the board wanted a change. It is perhaps worth noting that certain rumors claimed that La Follette was under pressure from "powerful elements" in the faculty to remove Frank.

[3] Frank wrote a letter of praise to Senator Robert La Follette, Jr., at the same time he was busy rallying support against Philip La Follette. Frank said, "You're doing a great job. Sincerity and grasp are evident in everything you do. I hope you live to be a hundred and stay at your post until the end." Frank to Robert La Follette, Jr., March 7, 1936, in the President's Papers.

[4] *Wisconsin State Journal*, March 11, 1936.

[5] *Ibid.*, May 12, June 15, 16, July 26, August 23, September 25, November 8, 1936.

[6] *Ibid.*, December 9, 1936; Sellery, *Some Ferments at Wisconsin*, 92.

[7] The exact reasons for Grady's shift are unclear, although he may have been motivated by political considerations. He was known to covet the governorship and may have been more interested in embarrassing La Follette than in helping Frank. In any event, Frank had given Grady advice in the spring of 1936 on how to unseat La Follette. Frank to Daniel Grady, June 8, 1936, in the Frank Papers.

[8] *Wisconsin State Journal*, December 15, 16, 1936.

[9] *Ibid.*, December 17, 1936.

[10] *Ibid.*, December 13, 30; *Antigo Journal*, December 14; *Milwaukee Journal*, December 17; *Ashland Press*, December 17, 1936.

[11] The complete transcript of the proceedings, together with a great deal of descriptive material, can be found in *Wisconsin State Journal*, January 6, 7, 8, 1937. There is also a transcript in the President's Papers. Elaborate accounts of the hearing appeared in all major Wisconsin newspapers. For instance, see *Capital Times, Milwaukee Journal, Milwaukee Sentinel,* and *Wisconsin State Journal*, all for January 6, 7, 8, 1937.

[12] Frank knew that La Follette had failed to get President James Conant of Harvard University to conduct a survey of the University of Wisconsin. According to one account, La Follette wrote Conant on December 21, 1936. Conant, in his reply dated December 24, 1936, stated, "The problem seems to me to be whether or not this present board of regents has the capacity, competence and independence to make the judgment free from prejudice of a political or personal nature." *Wisconsin State Journal*, January 8, 1937.

[13] Although Frank was suspended from his duties, he continued to receive his salary until his appointment officially expired at the conclusion of the academic year.

[14] *Wisconsin State Journal*, and *Capital Times*, both for January 8, 1937.

[15] *Wisconsin State Journal*, January 9; *Capital Times*, January 8, 1937.

[16] Mrs. Otto Falk, Alanson Houghton, and Harry Bullis to Frank, January 9, 10, in the Frank Papers; *Capital Times*, January 8, 9, 1937. Very few of Frank's old friends in New York from his *Century* days came to his defense either before or after his removal, although Hamilton Holt, then president of Rollins College, offered "friendship and support." Hamilton Holt to Frank, December 31, 1936, in the Frank Papers. More typical, however, was the attitude which Oswald Garrison Villard expressed in an article which

appeared not long before the hearing. Villard wrote, "It is true also that just because he is not a trained scholar his intercourse with the faculty has been limited; I think that he and his wife are frankly more interested in men and women of affairs and social distinction than in their own faculty. It is undeniable that they made tactical social mistakes in going to Madison and that the community gained the impression that President Frank felt that for him the University of Wisconsin was to be only a stepping stone to a higher sphere of activity." Oswald Garrison Villard, "Issues and Men," in *The Nation,* 143:762 (December 26, 1936).

¹⁷ University of Wisconsin *Faculty Minutes,* January 11, 1937.

¹⁸ *Ibid.* Sellery entitled Chapter Ten of his memoirs, *Some Ferments at Wisconsin,* "The Glenn Frank Regime."

CHAPTER X

¹ Frank to Herbert Hoover, May 4, 1929, January 17, 1930, in the President's Papers.

² Theodore Roosevelt, Jr., to Frank, October 29, 1934, and Robert R. McCormick to Frank, August 3, 1931, in the Glenn Frank Papers. Alfred Sloan, Jr., to Frank, June 4, 1934, in the President's Papers. For other reactions, see six bound volumes of correspondence addressed to Frank, 1931-1936, in the Frank Papers.

³ Frank to Robert Vanderpoll, November 27, 1934, in the President's Papers.

⁴ Glenn Frank, editorials entitled "Fighting a New Feudalism," February 26, 1930, and "Business Goes Bolshevik," October 31, 1930, in the Frank Papers.

⁵ Glenn Frank, *Thunder and Dawn,* 387. See also, Glenn Frank, editorial entitled "America's Destiny," January 1, 1931, in the Frank Papers.

⁶ Glenn Frank, editorials entitled "Roosevelt and the New Economics," September 29, 1933, "Private Initiative's Fate at Stake in Washington," May 5, 1933, "To Doubters of the New Deal," September 2, 1933, "Concentration of Power in President May Humanize Government," May 12, 1933, "If We Could Make it Unanimous," October 13, 1933, "The Heart of Recovery," September 6, 1933, "Between the NRA Lines," September 8, 1933, "Is the NRA Premature?", October 3, 1933, and "Toward Strikeless Industry," October 27, 1933, in *ibid.* See also, the *Boston Transcript,* October 26, 1933.

⁷ James E. Thompson to Frank, June 1, Frank to Thompson, June 21, July 13, and Frank to Martin Foss, August 29, 1934, in the Frank Papers.

⁸ Glenn Frank, *America's Hour of Decision* (New York, 1934), 226-227. A summary of the reviews of the book appeared in the *Wisconsin State Journal,* October 7, 1934. There is a folder labeled, "Important Letters About Mr. Frank's Book, *America's Hour of Decision,*" in the Frank Papers.

⁹ Glenn Frank, editorials entitled "The Cry for Security," February 1, 1935, "The Breeding of Dinosaurs," June 1, 1935, "The First Funeral on the Last Frontier," July 15, 1935, "Party Realism Again Possible," July 17, 1935, "A Doubting Thomas Doubts," August 13, 1936, in *ibid.*

[10] Glenn Frank, "If Business is Wise," June 3, 1935, and "The Supreme Court is Right," January 24, 1935, in *ibid.*; Glenn Frank, "The Conquest of Insecurity," in *Vital Speeches,* 1:285 (January 28, 1935).

[11] Frank to Edward Oldham, August 24, 1936, Frank to Kent County, Michigan Republican Committee, December 2, 1935, in the President's Papers. A newspaper reporter described the kind of entertainment that Frank provided for his guests. "Every June, Dr. and Mrs. Frank give a week-end house party at their home in Madison. . . . The Frank week-ends generally begin with Sunday luncheons, with guests assembling at a long table and spending several hours in lunching and conversation. Afterward there are walks through the gardens, never more beautiful than at this time of year, and discussions of events of the moment, particularly penetrating against the serenity of the surroundings. Visitors who wish to see the university may do so and members of the faculty frequently arrive for tea or dinner." *Chicago Daily News,* June 24, 1935, in the Frank Papers.

[12] *Wisconsin State Journal,* May 23, 1935. For a comment on Frank's possibilities as a candidate, see Raymond Clapper, "Where Will Lightning Strike?" in the *Review of Reviews,* 91:29 (May, 1935).

[13] Frank Vanderlip to Frank, March 11, 1935, in the Frank Papers.

[14] *Wisconsin State Journal,* August 28, 1935. Still, Frank was concerned about his role in national politics early the next year. After visiting with the Franks, Margaret Ayer Barnes, a Pulitzer prize-winning novelist, wrote Frank, "I loved staying with you and I loved the concert and the tea parties and the superb midnight supper—but most of all I loved hearing you and Glenn talk over the state of the nation, and the state of the Frank family— so closely intermingled. I keep thinking of Glenn's dilemma—can't get it out of my mind. . . . Well, it's all very exciting and I shall be eager to hear Glenn's decision. I feel I went up to Madison to put my finger on the pulse of the nation! I'm all agog over it. . . . Still think of Glenn walking round and round in mental circles with his problem."

[15] Typescript manuscript entitled "Rural Progress, Inc.," in the Frank Papers.

[16] Frank to "Stockholders," June 30, 1937, in *ibid.* See also, "Memorandum of Agreement, Rural Progress, Inc.," June 30, 1937, in *ibid.* Frank discontinued his daily newspaper column at the time he became connected with *Rural Progress.*

[17] *Rural Progress* to "1500 Advertisers," July 22, 1937, in *ibid.*

[18] Maurice Reynolds, "Straight Across the Fence," in *Rural Progress,* D:3 (September, 1937).

[19] Glenn Frank, "Since I cannot Visit With You," in *Rural Progress,* D:3 (October, 1937).

[20] Glenn Frank, "Scarcity is Not a Savior," in *Rural Progress,* D:3 (November, 1937).

[21] The *Wisconsin State Journal,* May 6, 8, 1938, carried detailed information on the investigation. The committee listed the backers of *Rural Progress* as follows: Charles Albright of Milwaukee, $25,000; Chicago Rotoprint, $107,000; George Ball of Muncie, Indiana, $6,250; Frank Barron of Milwaukee, $10,000; Carnation Co., $10,000; Herman Falk of Milwaukee, $10,000; Otto Falk of Milwaukee, $10,000; Alfred Kieckhefer of Milwaukee, $5,000; George Mead of Wisconsin Rapids, $10,000; Maurice Reynolds of Chicago, $90,000; Edward

Rumely of Chicago, $12,500; Frank Vanderlip, Jr., of New York City, $3,750; Estate of Frank Vanderlip, $10,000; and others, $12,500. If the committee report was correct Frank invested no money of his own.

[22] Edward Rumely to Frank, May 9, 1938, in the Frank Papers.

[23] "Memorandum," Frank to Republican National Committee, probably February or March, 1940, in *ibid.*

[24] Herbert Hoover to Glenn Frank, October 2, 1937, in *ibid.*

[25] Frank to John Hamilton, January 5, 1938, in *ibid.*

[26] John Hamilton to Frank, January 18, 1939, in *ibid.*

[27] Report of the Republican Program Committee, *A Program for A Dynamic America, A Statement of Republican Principles* (no place, 1940), 2.

[28] *Wisconsin State Journal,* March 4, 1940.

[29] *Ibid.,* July 31, 1940.

[30] Glenn Frank, editorial entitled "The Anatomy of Failure," November 16, 1925, in the Frank Papers. Frank, in spite of the thousands upon thousands of dollars he earned in his lifetime, left a very modest estate. The clear market value of his estate was $74,646.03, but had he not left a $77,996.03 trust fund he would have died in debt. See, Tax Order, January 17, 1942, in Dane County Court, Inheritance Tax Orders, Series 013/10/10–1, 12:377, at the State Historical Society of Wisconsin.

SOURCES

THE MATERIAL used in this study was accumulated over a period of several years. The bulk of it is from manuscript and archival sources. Various newspapers were combed for information, as were numerous books and articles. The author also interviewed several people associated with politics and education in Wisconsin in the 1930's, and drew upon knowledge that he acquired while working as a graduate assistant in the University of Wisconsin Archives. All the pertinent sources have been cited in full in the notes to the text. The following essay on sources is highly selective, and is intended to give an indication of the materials which were found to be most helpful.

The basic manuscript collection is the Glenn Frank Papers, housed in the Glenn Frank Room of the library at Northeast Missouri State Teachers College, Kirksville, Missouri. The bulk of the Frank Papers consists of over fifty file drawers of incoming and outgoing correspondence, most of which dates from before 1925 and after 1937. Included are correspondence with famous literary and political figures, routine business letters, personal letters, bound volumes of letters commenting on Frank's speeches and writings, and special files of correspondence that Frank considered especially important. There are also bound volumes of Frank's speeches, a complete file of his newspaper columns, reprints of most of the articles which he wrote, photographs, a file of clippings, family records, memorabilia, and a large library that he collected. The Frank Papers are unarranged and hence difficult to use.

An invaluable archival series, Presidents of the University,

General Correspondence, Series 4/11/1, at the University of Wisconsin Archives, contains incoming and outgoing correspondence for Frank's years as president of the University, 1925 to 1937. The correspondence for his tenure comprises more than sixty cubic feet. Much of it is routine, but it contains major administrative papers, confidential reports, transcripts of hearings, and the like. Moreover, it includes the great bulk of Frank's personal correspondence for the period. The series is arranged alphabetically by year.

Material covering Frank's days at Northwestern University, first as a student and then as alumni secretary, can be found in the University of Northwestern Archives. These include the Northwestern Board of Trustees' Minutes, Northwestern Alumni Association Minutes, Glenn Frank Folder, and the papers of Abram W. Harris and James Alton James. At the State Historical Society of Wisconsin the William Burnette Papers, Zona Gale Papers, John Hicks Papers concerning Glenn Frank, Edward Kremers Papers, Theodore Kronshage Papers, and Michael Olbrich Papers all contain material dealing with various phases of Frank's administration of the University of Wisconsin. There are numerous archival series at the University of Wisconsin Archives besides the presidents' correspondence which cover Frank's administration. The most basic of these are President's Papers, General Subject Files (B. Series), Series 4/0/1, which has a file of newspaper clippings; Board of Regents Minutes, Series 1/1/1, which contains the formal minutes of meetings; and Board of Regents, Secretary, Miscellaneous Alphabetical File, Series 1/1/2, which is the correspondence file for the Board.

Two Madison newspapers, the *Capital Times* and the *Wisconsin State Journal,* covered the affairs of the University of Wisconsin in detail. Two Wisconsin metropolitan papers, the *Milwaukee Journal* and the *Milwaukee Sentinel,* also have much information about the University. The *Daily Northwestern* and the *Daily Cardinal,* student newspapers at Northwestern and Wisconsin respectively, have some valuable information not found elsewhere. Material by and about Glenn Frank can be found in many American newspapers; his daily column appeared regularly for a twelve-year period in several dozen papers.

Merle Curti and Vernon Carstensen, *The University of Wisconsin* (2 vols., Madison, 1949), provides valuable insight into the affairs of the University prior to Frank's presidency. Frederick Rosentreter, *The Boundaries of the Campus* (Madison, 1957), has a chapter on the Extension Division during Frank's tenure. The most valuable memoir is that of George Sellery, *Some Ferments at Wisconsin, 1901–1947, Memories and Reflections* (Madison, 1960). Curiously, the Sellery Papers in the University of Wisconsin Archives have little on the dean's relationship with Frank. For very unfavorable views of Frank's presidency, see John Chapple, *La Follette Socialism* (Ashland, Wisconsin, 1931) and *La Follette Road to Communism* (Ashland, Wisconsin, 1936), and Ernest Meyer, "Glenn Frank: Journalist on Parole," in the *American Mercury,* 31:149 (January, 1934). A very useful appraisal of Frank's career is *In Appreciation of Glenn Frank: Proceedings of the First Annual Wisconsin X Club Banquet Upon the Occasion of the Presentation of the Glenn Frank Memorial Portrait to the University of Wisconsin* (Madison, 1941).

Finally, Glenn Frank's own writings were a prime source for this biography. He wrote a tremendous amount during his lifetime. His books, *Stakes of the War,* co-authored with Lothrop Stoddard (New York, 1918); *The Politics of Industry* (New York, 1919); *An American Looks at His World* (New York, 1923); *Thunder and Dawn* (New York, 1932); and *America's Hour of Decision* (New York, 1934) enumerate most of his basic ideas. His daily columns, his editorials in the *Century Magazine* and *Rural Progress,* and his numerous articles were invaluable.

INDEX

ADDAMS, Jane: member of League to Enforce Peace, 32
Agricultural Extension Division: 75
Agriculture Hall: 120
Alber, Louis: Frank's agent, 44
Albright, Charles: *Rural Progress* backer, 186*n*
American Mercury: article critical of Frank, 135; article defending Frank, 136
America's Hour of Decision: written by Frank, 154, 157-158
An American Looks at His World: written by Frank, 43
Athletics: controversy over, 113-115

BALL, George: *Rural Progress* backer, 162, 186*n*
Bardeen, Charles: dean of University medical school, 75
Barron, Frank: *Rural Progress* backer, 186*n*
Birge, Edward A.: University president, 49; retirement plans, 50; administration described, 64; promises co-operation with Frank, 66; Sellery advises, 76; Frank's attitude toward, 80; mentioned, 53, 82
Board of Regents: establishes academic freedom, 47; searches for president, 50-53; considers Frank, 54; hires Frank, 63-65; composition, 73-74; problem of accepting private funds, 81-83; attitude toward Frank's syndicated column, 94; approves salary waiver, 107-108; involved in University problems, 112-114; manner appointed, 139; possibility of Frank's ouster, 140-141; plans for ouster, 142-143; ouster hearing, 144-148
Board of Visitors: characterized, 75; urges University changes, 90
Boston, Massachusetts: Frank moves to, 27; characterized, 36; mentioned, 24-95 *passim*
Burnette, William: investigates University, 117-119; mentioned, 121, 138
Butler, Henry: member of Board of Regents, 50; on nominating committee, 50

CALLAHAN, John: member of Board of Regents, 50; on nominating committee, 50; meets Edward A. Filene, 52; favors Frank's candidacy, 63; negotiates with Frank, 140; involved in Frank's ouster, 140; at ouster hearing, 144
Capital Times: praises Frank, 65; voice of progressives, 72; comments on Frank's role as president, 72; hails rejection of private funds, 82; approves Frank's ouster, 149
Carnation Co.: *Rural Progress* backer, 186*n*
Century Company: publishes *The Stakes of the War,* 32; characterized, 37
Century Magazine: background of, 37; Frank becomes associate editor, 38-39; Frank becomes editor-in-chief, 39-40; Frank edits, 40-41; Frank's editorship evaluated, 45
Chapple, John: characterized, 116; writes *La Follette Socialism,* 116; attacks University, 117; runs for Senate, 117; comments on ouster proceedings, 144; mentioned, 118, 121, 138
Chautauqua circuit: 20
Chicago Rotoprint: *Rural Progress* backer, 186*n*
Chicago Tribune: critical of Frank, 89; on Experimental College, 100; publisher approves of Frank speech, 154

ations of office, 96–97; lobbying,
97–98; establishes Experimental
College, 99; criticized by Sellery,
102–103; takes credit for University's progress, 106; salary waiver
controversy, 107–108; position
damaged by actions in Rocking
Chair Scandal, 109–112; hurt by
internal controversies, 114–115;
contends with charges of University's "radicalism," 115–119; de-
fends academic freedom, 120–121;
fails to remove Sellery, 122–123;
relations with La Follette family,
123; breaks with Philip La Follette, 123–124, relations with legislature, 124–125; attacked by
Meyer, 126, 135–136; defended by
Zona Gale, 136; evaluation of administration, 136–138; e v e n t s
move toward removal as president, 139–148; ousted as University president, 148; receives expressions of support, 150; Sellery
characterizes Frank administration, 150–151; why Frank fought
removal, 152–153; political aspirations, 153–154; comments on problems of Great Depression, 155–
156; writes *Thunder and Dawn*,
156; attacks New Deal, 157–158;
writes *America's Hour of Decision*, 158; becomes anti-New Deal
spokesman, 158–160; seen as possible presidential candidate, 160–
161; acquires *Rural Progress*,
161–164; offers *Rural Progress* to
Republican Party, 165; failure
of *Rural Progress*, 165; heads
R.P.C., 165–167; issues *A Program
for Dynamic America*, 167–168;
at 1940 Republican National
Convention, 168; enters Wisconsin senatorial primary, 169; career
evaluated, 169–170. *Views:* on
rural life, 8–9; on Billy Sunday,
13; on advertising, 17–18; on religion, 19; on machine age, 19–20,
42, 91–92; on undergraduate
studies, 21; on importance of for-

eign affairs, 32; on modern industrialism, 33–34; on nationalism, 42; on popular government,
42; on influence of religion, 42;
on "Spiritual Renaissance," 42;
on business leadership, 42; on
career in education, 53; on University of Wisconsin, 68; on role
of college president, 71, 72, 73,
80, 81, 95, 96–97; on Americanism, 72; on philosophy of life,
72–73; on political dominance of
universities, 83; on educational
change, 84–85, 90, 92; on academic freedom, 90, 120–121; on future
of western civilization, 92; on Experimental College curriculum,
100; on discipline, 111; on athletic controversy, 115; on need to
reorganize University, 122; on
liberalism, 135–136; on La Follette family, 124; on Philip Fox
La Follette, 140; on administrative accomplishments, 146–147; on
Herbert Hoover, 153–154; on
causes of Great depression, 155–
156; on New Deal, 156–157, 159;
on individualism, 155–156; on
farm programs, 164; role as R.P.C.
chairman, 166
Frank, Glenn, Jr.: 3, 5, 35, 70, 88,
95, 175n
Frank, Gordon: father of Glenn
Frank, 9
Frank, Mary (Smith): learns of accident, 6; courted, 34; background, 34–35; marries Frank, 35;
lives in Boston, 35–36; arrives in
Madison, 70; Madison social
leader, 95; rumored social break
with La Follettes, 124; rumors
about, 126
Frank, Nancy Hombs: mother of
Glenn Frank, 9

GALE, Zona: *Century* contributor,
40; visits Frank, 44; writes Frank
concerning University presidency,
46, 49; member of Board of Regents, 47; evaluation of, 47; mem-